D0856204

What Does the Old Testament Say About God?

What Does the Old Testament Say About God?

By
CLAUS WESTERMANN

Edited by Friedemann W. Golka

JOHN KNOX PRESS
ATLANTA

Library of Congress Cataloging in Publication Data

Westermann, Claus.
   What does the Old Testament say about God?

   "Based on the Sprunt lectures delivered . . . at Union Theological Seminary, Richmond, Virginia, from January 31 to February 3, 1977."
   Includes bibliographical references.
     1. God—Biblical teaching. 2. Bible. N.T.
—Relation to the Old Testament. 3. Jesus Christ—Person and offices. I. Golka, Friedemann W. II. Title.
BS1192.6.W47   231   78-52448
ISBN 0–8042–0190–0

© 1979 John Knox Press

Printed in the United States of America

Editor's Preface

This book is based on the Sprunt Lectures delivered by Professor D. Claus Westermann at Union Theological Seminary, Richmond, Virginia, from January 31 to February 3, 1977. The first four lectures, which have been translated by Julian Grinsted and the present editor, appear more or less in their original form with the addition of bibliographical material. The two final lectures (chapters V and VI) have been thoroughly revised and retranslated by the Reverend Alastair H. B. Logan and the present editor. I am also greatly indebted to my colleague Alastair Logan for taking upon himself the labor of proofreading.

Last, but by no means least, thanks must go to Lady Frances M. Bruce Lockhart for her perseverance in typing not only the original lectures, but also the version presented in this book.

Friedemann W. Golka
University of Exeter, Devon, U. K.
May 1978

Contents

8

I

What Does
the Old Testament
Say About God?

Introduction[1]

What does the Old Testament say about God? The answer to this question has to be given from the Old Testament in its entirety. It is the task of a theology of the Old Testament to describe and view together what the Old Testament as a whole, in all its sections, says about God.[2] The task is not correctly understood if one takes one part of the Old Testament to be the most important and gives it prominence over the others; or if one regards the whole as determined by one concept such as covenant or election or salvation; or if one asks, to begin with, what the theological center of the Old Testament is. The New Testament obviously has its center in the suffering, death, and resurrection of Christ, to which the Gospels are directed and which the Epistles take as their starting point. The Old Testament, however, has no similarity at all to this structure. It is therefore not possible to translate the problem of the theological center from the New to the Old Testament.[3]

If we wish to describe what the Old Testament as a whole says about God, we have to start by looking at the way in which the Old Testament presents itself; this can be recognized by everyone: "The

Old Testament tells a story" (Gerhard von Rad). With that statement we have reached our first decision about the form of an Old Testament theology: if the Old Testament narrates what it has to say about God in the form of a story, then the structure of an Old Testament theology must be based on events rather than concepts.[4]

But how can we define this structure of events more exactly? There seems to be an obvious answer to this question: the task of a theology of the Old Testament could simply consist of re-narrating the story of the Old Testament in an abbreviated and summarized form. This was certainly how Gerhard von Rad understood it: "Re-telling the story is therefore still the most legitimate way for theology to speak about the Old Testament."[5] This would be possible if the whole of the Old Testament consisted of a continuous story from the first to the last chapter. However, this is not the case.[6]

The Old Testament has come down to us in a threefold structure, in which it also originated: the Torah, the Prophets, and the Writings; or the historical, prophetic, and didactic books, the nucleus of which is the Psalms. The Bible of the Old Testament, according to this conception of the traditionists, consists, apart from the narrative, of the word of God, which occurs in the events, and of humanity's response in calling to God. The narrative of the historical books from Genesis to Chronicles does contain texts in which the word of God enters the action, and texts which contain the response of praise or lament. But the structure of the Old Testament in its three parts indicates that the narrative in the Old Testament is determined by the word of God occurring in it and by the response of those for whom God acts and with whom he deals.

It is therefore the canon of the Old Testament itself which shows us the structure of what happens in the Old Testament in its decisive elements.[7] We have thus found an objective starting point for an Old Testament theology which is independent of any preconceptions about what the most important thing in the Old Testament is and independent of any other prior theological decisions. If one asks what the Old Testament says about God, this threefold structure shows us the way to the answer.

But how can what the Old Testament says about God be viewed and described together in its many and diverse forms? How can it be expressed along broad and simple lines? In previous Old Testament theologies this has been attempted predominantly by reducing what the Old Testament says about God to comprehensive terms such as salvation, election, covenant, faith, kerygma, revelation, redemption, soteriology, eschatology, etc. By using these noun concepts they moved away from the language of the Old Testament, which is overwhelmingly dominated by verbs; in addition this meant a loss of the diversity in which the Old Testament speaks of God.[8]

If we wish to clarify these broad lines that determine the whole way in which the Old Testament speaks of God and yet not overlook the many forms in which it occurs, we shall therefore have to start from verb structures. This demands a complete change in our way of thinking. Instead of looking at the Word of God for its thought-content, we shall have to approach it as an *action* between God and people and determine its functions. Instead of looking for a state of salvation, we shall have to look for an act of saving, and so on.

The large contexts of the Old Testament have to be understood by starting from these verb structures. In the historical books just such a large context is apparently provided by the relationship of the Pentateuch to the Deuteronomistic History Work: in the middle of the one stands the confession of praise,[9] in the middle of the other the confession of sin.[10] A further theologically significant context is provided by the three-part structure of the Yahwistic Work: primeval history, patriarchal history, and history of the people. The Priestly Code is determined by a basic structure according to which everything that happens results from the commanding word of God and its obedient execution.[11] In the prophetic books the question of the message of the prophets has to start from the prophetic oracle of judgment, which is common to all prophets. It is therefore a constant factor, from which the varying individual expressions of the prophetic message have to be understood.[12] In the Psalms this constant factor is given by the structure of the Psalms of lament and praise, from which can be understood both the varying individual expressions and any subordinate forms of these Psalms.[13]

So far we have only hinted at a few main features. They should show that from such a starting point of an Old Testament theology,[14] the whole of what the Old Testament says about God can be expressed along a few simple lines, without losing sight of the many and diverse forms of the statements of the Old Testament about God. The theology of the Old Testament thus remains determined in every aspect by the outline of a story, which has been entrusted to us, and to which belong the occurrence of God speaking and the response of those who experience these events.

A. The History

1. Old Testament Theology and Historical Science

What kind of story does the Old Testament tell? It differs from history, as understood by modern historical science, in that what happens happens between God and humanity, between the creator and his creation. The nineteenth-century concept of history cannot be applied to an Old Testament theology authoritatively because it excludes an act of God as an integral part of history *a priori*. In the Old Testament, God's acts and words belong to all events; reality without the working of God does not exist for Old Testament people. What moves history takes place between God and humans; this is what Martin Buber calls an event in dialogue.[15] This has its roots in the creation of man; God has created man in his image, to correspond with him, so that something may happen between him and this creature.[16]

The discussion on the problem of whether Old Testament theology should be concerned with history as it can be demonstrated in certain events, or whether with the conceptions of Israel's faith about this history, this discussion, which began between Gerhard von Rad and Franz Hesse, started from false presuppositions on both sides.[17] What the Old Testament says about reality, it says about God; what it says about God, it says about reality.

This gives a broad horizon to the story told by the Old Testament. To speak of God means to speak of the whole of reality. With the very first words of the Bible: "In the beginning . . . God created the heavens and the earth," the Old Testament shatters our distinction between nature and history. Because God is at work in everything, human history enters the broader horizon of natural history from its beginning to its end. It follows from the creation of the world that every-thing created remains in God's hands, " 'While the earth remains . . .' " (Gen. 8:22); it follows from the creation of man that God's acts embrace the history of the whole of humanity.

The history of which the Old Testament tells occurs simultane-ously in three circles: near the center it is the history of the people of God, which corresponds to the political history of one nation among other nations, and which can be historically represented; in a larger circle it is the history of the human family, of generations of families in their personal, completely a-political sphere of life, as it is depicted in the patriarchal history; in the largest circle it is the history of humanity as a whole, divided into nations, on the earth as a whole, as it is the subject of the primeval history at the beginning and of apocalyptic at the end. This is the concept of the Yahwist, which is apparent in his combination of the primeval history (Gen. 1—11) with the patriarchal history (Gen. 12—50) and with the history of the people (from the exodus to the conquest of Canaan). It is clear-ly manifested in the introduction to the patriarchal history (Gen. 12:1–3), in which the promise of Abraham is not limited to Israel, the people of God, but, looking back to the nations into which humanity branched out (Gen. 10), the promise of blessing includes the nations of the earth: " 'by you all the families of the earth shall bless them-selves.' " (Gen. 12:3)

2. Old Testament Theology and Salvation History

The concept of salvation history, which was coined in the nine-teenth century and which was dependent on that century's under-standing of history, cannot, at least not alone, fully contain a theology of the Old Testament.[18] As opposed to a narrow concept of salvation history, the Old Testament speaks of an event between God and men, which is not limited to a history of God's acts of salvation. Yes, the history of the people of Israel begins with a divine act of salvation, and the confession of God as the savior remains decisive right into the New Testament. In regard to those facts, one can speak with good reason of a salvation history; but the working of God for his people is not confined to his acts of salvation; his saving is contrasted with his judgment. But neither does this history speak only of God as saving and judging; it also speaks of God as blessing, and this blessing has from the very beginning a universal aspect. In the structure of the Pentateuch, the complementary relationship of God's saving and blessing can be demonstrated by the fact that the center, Exodus to Numbers, speaks of God's saving, while the framework, Genesis and Deuteronomy, speaks predominantly of God's blessing. The Old Testament speaks differently of the blessing and saving acts of God: the latter consist of individual acts, the former are a continuous action consisting of the power of fertility, nourishment, growth, and support. In the blessing, the working of the creator (Gen. 1:28) reaches into the present of each generation.

The specific character of history, as told in the Old Testament, consists of the fact that the working of God from beginning to end is not related to the same entity, i. e., the nation, but embraces in a universal concept all important forms of community in human history, in the center of which stand the people of God and their history: family, tribe, nation, and the cultic congregation. All areas of human life participate in this history: economy, culture, politics, and social life. All of these spheres belong somewhere in what happens between God and humanity, but they are of necessity different as they appear in a family, in a tribe in the process of settlement, in a village community with agriculture, and at a royal court. Consequently, everything which the Old Testament says about God in all these situations must be different. In this process everything has its meaning and its necessity: what the patriarchs experienced on their wanderings and in their families about and with God; the exodus group from Egypt at the Reed Sea, in the wilderness, and at Sinai; the experience of the immigrating tribes in their struggles for a settlement; the new experiences of the call of a leader; the encounter with the sanctuaries of the inhabitants of Canaan; the experience of God's blessing in the new form of economy, i. e., agriculture, with its annual feasts; the adoption of kingship with new promises and new dangers right up to the suffering through the collapse of the two kingdoms, which had been announced long before by the prophets, and on up to the humiliations of the exile and the new beginning of the temple congregation in the province of an Oriental empire. This diverse reality in its multitude of forms of presentation is embraced by the working of God, moved by the word of God, and causing a response.

B. The Word of God in the Old Testament

The second part of the canon, the Prophets, has as its actual subject matter the occurrence of the word of God, in which the words of the individual prophets are presented in the context of the historical process in which they occur.

But it is not only this part of the canon that deals with the word of God; on the contrary, the word of God belongs in all sorts of forms to everything that the Old Testament says about God. The significance of God for his people consists of both his working and his word together.

1. Two Ways of Understanding "Word"

But what does the "word" of God mean in the Old Testament? It is here not primarily understood on the basis of its content, but as an action which takes place between a speaker and a listener. The word's purpose is to reach the listener and cause a response. Understood in this manner, the word of God in its many expressions belongs to the history which is told in the first part of the canon.

In modern theology "word of God" is to a large extent understood differently from the way it is meant in the Old Testament; modern theology understands it on the basis of its content: the word of God is the content of what God has said.[19] As such it can be found as given and become the subject of reflection. The word of God becomes separated from the process of its occurrence, and therefore an objective entity at scholars' disposal, material with which the scholar can work. But every word of God, whatever it says and however it occurs, has a function in what happens between God and humanity. Taken out of this context, it ceases to be the word of God.

2. Three Main Functions of the Word

We can distinguish three main functions of the word of God: announcement, instruction or directive, and the word in the context of worship.

a. The Word as Announcement

The word as announcement has its center in prophecy, but is not confined to it. Because of its character it is necessarily two-sided; it announces salvation or it announces doom, either as promise or as an announcement of judgment. Both belong together throughout the Old Testament, from the primeval history right up to apocalyptic. Both have a wealth of forms and can occur in many different situations. Summarized they can only be represented by a history of the promises[20] and a history of the words of judgment throughout the Old Testament.

b. The Word as Instruction

The word of God also appears as instruction (torah). Later, this comes to be described in summary form as Law; but the different designations in Deuteronomy (commandments, statutes, and laws) indicate that the overriding concept of Law embraces different forms and processes. Commandment (prohibition) and law are basically different processes. The commandment or prohibition consists of only one sentence in the form of a direct address; the law is expressed in one sentence with two parts, connecting the deed with its consequence. The law presupposes an institution which has the power to punish and make decisions; the authority of the commandment is that of the God who gave it. Closely related to the commandment is the exhortation (and warning), above all in the deuteronomic paraenesis, which sets out a positive or negative consequence in the form of a conditional clause. Commandments and laws belonged originally to different life situations and have been transmitted in different ways: in series of commandments and legal corpora. Only afterwards did they come together in the legal collections of the Pentateuch, and only at that point did the "Law" arise, which comprises commandments (exhortations) and many sorts of laws. In this combined form they have become part of the Sinai theophany and the Law which God has given his people.

But in the Old Testament the word of God as instruction is not confined to the series of commandments and legal corpora. It also includes commissions, orders, and commands throughout the entire Old Testament in the flow of daily life, from the prohibition against eating the fruit of the tree in the middle of the garden on up to the commissions and commands to a prophet and other commanding and instructing words of God in all writings of the Old Testament. These instructions or directives are given to an individual in a certain situation and are confined to the situation, e.g., the command to Abraham: " 'Go out from your father's house.' " (Gen. 12:1, author's translation; cf. 46:1–3) The commandment is totally different; it applies to everyone and for all time, as, e. g., " 'You shall have no other gods before me.' " This kind of commandment, since it applies to everyone and for all time, could, therefore, attached to the cult, become an integral part of worship.

c. The Cultic Word

The cultic word has its place in the context of a sacred act—it presupposes the assembly of the congregation for worship and the existence of a cult-mediator (priest). But in the cult itself the cultic word has different functions. To the cultic word, in particular, belong the pronouncement of forgiveness or of favorable hearing (which is stated in the past tense), the distribution of blessing, and the proclamation of the commandments. Corresponding to the cultic word are the liturgical answer of the congregation, the Amen, the praise of God, the sacrificial saying, and the confession. The cultic word as directed to the people and the liturgical response of the people come together in the act of worship.

This cultic word has to be distinguished from the word of God which occurs to an individual or to a group of people in the flow of everyday life, for instance, when Abraham, having raised the knife, hears a voice: " 'Do not lay your hand on the lad' " (Gen. 22:12); or when the call occurs to a group threatened by a more powerful enemy: "Do not be . . . afraid" (Deut. 1:29); or when David hears the word from the mouth of Nathan: " 'You are the man!' " (2 Sam. 12:7) The word as spoken and heard in worship is distinguished from these examples above all by the fact that those who come together at a particular place and at a particular time come together in the readiness to listen to the word of God and the holy time and the holy place form a space of calmness (Exod. 24:15–18), which promotes this readiness to listen.

The word of God which occurs in worship is at the same time the word that has been transmitted or handed down.[21] In the act of worship, protected and secured by the particular time and place, it is received and handed down from generation to generation. But this word of God which is transmitted in the cult, secured by the institution, and preserved unchanged by this holy act, would become fossilized if it did not also stand in a lively, alternating relationship with the word of God as it occurs and is listened to outside worship in the flow of daily life. Only these two together form the word of God, never the one without the other.

3. Revelation in the Old Testament

We spoke about the acts of God and the words of God. How is the concept of revelation related to them? The Old Testament does not have a general concept of revelation.[22] Instead of such a general concept there are special occurrences in the Old Testament of God's acting and God's speaking. The God who *speaks* to his people or to an individual reveals himself differently from the God who is *acting* for his people or for an individual. There are therefore two different types of revelation in the Old Testament: the saving acts of God, which are connected with the epiphany or God's coming; and the word of God, which is connected with the theophany. These are two different processes and one can follow the history of both through the whole Old Testament.[23]

The saving God is the coming God. Revealing himself has here the same sense as coming. In every case it is coming into a situation of distress. In earlier times this is represented as an advent of God which shakes the cosmos with tremendous uproar in nature, as for example in connection with the deliverance from Egypt or in the time of the Judges at the beginning of the Song of Deborah (Judg. 5:4–5). Later on it is the judging, punishing God who comes to judge his people in such an epiphany; and at the end it is God's coming to judge the world in the apocalyptic writings. In God's dealing with the individual this coming of God has its place in the Psalms of lament: the request for God's coming precedes the request for God's saving intervention. The saving God is the coming God.[24]

God's speaking is connected with the theophany, as represented, for example, in the Sinai theophany (Exod. 19—34).[25] Theophany differs from epiphany in that its goal is not the act but the word of God. The other difference is that only a theophany establishes a holy place. A holy place established by a theophany is also found in the patriarchal stories, e. g., in Genesis 28. In a changed form the theophany is met with in the call visions of the prophets.

But the Old Testament never speaks of revelation in connection with blessing or with creation. One cannot find anything in the Old Testament like revelation through creation *(revelatio generalis).*[26] God's quiet and continuous work of blessing does not need a revelation.

C. Humanity's Response

1. The Response in Words

God's work, at least in part, consists of his deeds and words; similarly, the human response is by word and action. Sometimes the human response in words happens as an immediate reaction in the flow of daily life, e. g., a shout of praise, a word of thanksgiving, or a vow.[27] Or the response may be the words directed to God in the sanctuary, the prayers and songs of worship, as transmitted in the Psalms. The whole history narrated in the Old Testament has the character of a dialogue; this alternating action between God and humans is particularly expressed by the fact that elements which appear in the historical books as immediate responses to the flow of daily life are canonized and fused together into a whole in the Psalms. All the individual components of a Psalm of lament—the call to God, the lament, the request, the vow—can also appear as components of a narrative, as in Jacob's vow (Gen. 28:20–22) or in the lament of Samson (Judg. 15:18). In all these cases the elements of prayer form a necessary part of the story, which would be incomplete without the human response. Therefore we have to regard the Psalms as simply the center of a history of prayer going through the Old Testament from beginning to end, from the lament of Cain to the praise of God in the apocalyptic. We can distinguish three stages in the history of prayer in the Old Testament: the very short words of prayer in the historical books, the central point—the prayers in the Psalms, and the long prayers in prose in the postexilic period.[28]

In the Psalms the two main groups, Psalms of praise and laments, correspond to the action of God in salvation and judgment, and the respective announcements. The experience of suffering is voiced in the lament directed to God, the experience of joy is voiced in the praise of God. Lament and praise are two poles, which comprise the whole of human existence. This polarity corresponds to human existence between birth and death, leading from heights to depths, from depths to heights.[29]

2. Humanity's Response in Action

People's response in action consists of the carrying out in everyday life of what they have been commanded to do, as well as the sacrifice, the specific act directed towards God at the sanctuary.

a. Carrying Out God's Commands

The historical books speak of the human response as everyday actions; in them the dominant pattern is that God commands something and it is carried out. The Old Testament presupposes that a person who has been commanded by God to do something is able to do it, and, under normal circumstances, would do it. When God commands Abraham " 'Go out . . .' " and it is then reported that "Abraham went . . . ," Abraham has thus complied with God's will. Even a pagan seer, Balaam, can do the will of God, when God commands him not to curse but to bless Israel. God's commandments are such that they comply with human capabilities: " 'For this commandment which I command you this day is not too hard for you, neither is it far off.' " (Deut. 30:11)[30] If this were not the case, it would be impossible to distinguish between obedience and disobedience, and it is the alternation between these that determines the entire course of Israel's history. The message of judgment and the accusation of the prophets only occur when the disobedience of the people has risen to such a level as to necessitate them. People's relationship to God in the Old Testament presupposes that they can say "Yes" to God and act according to this "Yes."

b. The Sacrifice

The specific act directed towards God in the context of worship, the sacrifice, has a fluctuating history in the Old Testament.[31] The primeval history presents sacrifice as necessary for human existence: in Genesis 4 as an immediate response to God's blessing; in Genesis 8:20–22 as a response to his saving. Here, as everywhere else in the Old Testament, the assumption is that sacrifice is a phenomenon of religion as a whole, and nothing which is peculiar to Israel's relationship to God. It has remained a decisive factor for the understanding of sacrifice in Israel that humans were created, not, as in the Babylonian creation myths, to serve the gods, but rather to be obedient to God's command, to cultivate and preserve the earth.[32] Consequently, in the Old Testament, sacrifice could never take the place of the observance of God's will in everyday life. The Old Testament emphasizes obedience as opposed to sacrifice—"Obedience is better than sacrifice"—but never the reverse. This enables the history between God and his people to continue, even when sacrifice has become impossible through the destruction of the temple.

Conclusion

We have seen that what is said about God in the Old Testament is a story or a history developing between God and man. As in all the stories of the world, there is on both sides action and reaction, word and response. The actions of God, the words of God, and the words and actions of men in response are the basic elements of the history of God and humanity, of God and his people.

But what is it that holds together all that is going on between God and humanity, what makes it into real history, into a story with beginning and end? It is the oneness of God. Israel confesses: Yahweh, our God, Yahweh is one. Because the creator is the same as the savior and the judge, because the saving God is the same as the blessing God, because there is only one to praise and only one to complain to, because there is only one to trust, therefore there is a connection, holding together all that is going on between God and humanity, therefore it is a real story with beginning and end. As God says in Deutero-Isaiah: " 'I am the first and I am the last.' " (Isa. 44:6)

Here we find a fundamental difference between Israel and its neighbors. If there are *many* gods, what is happening happens in the first place between the gods, between divine beings. If there is only *one* God, all that is happening takes place between this one God and his creation—including his people. The confession to the one God is a response to the work of the one God, work dedicated only to his creation and only to his people. Because he alone is God, he makes possible a history between God and the world beginning with God and ending with God: " 'I am the first and I am the last.' "[33]

II
The Saving God
and
History

A. The Experience of Being Saved

*1. God Was the Savior of Israel (The "Little Historic Creed":
Exodus)*

"The Old Testament tells a story" (von Rad); but the story which the Old Testament tells can be equated neither with the concept of history, which has developed from the Enlightenment and which received its decisive form in the nineteenth century, nor with a religious or salvation history, as opposed to profane history. We have to go back behind these alternatives to a broader concept of history, in which both have not yet been separated, one which is able to embrace historical as well as religious events, and which would be in this respect more appropriate to the way in which the Old Testament talks about history. The Old Testament reports what happens from God towards people and from people towards God; thus it embraces speaking and acting, words and acts, in both directions. Because all events are in a dialogue, they must have had their beginning in an encounter. This encounter the Old Testament describes as the exodus, with which the history of God with his people begins.[1]

This report of the saving from Egypt forms the nucleus of the Pentateuch, as the "little historic creed" (von Rad)[2] shows, which summarizes the reports of the book of Exodus in a few sentences, and therefore in its structure corresponds in broad outline to the structure of the whole book. The importance of this short summary of what God has done for Israel is shown by the fact that it is spoken in a fixed form both at the presentation of sacrifice (Deut. 26) and in parents' recitation to their children of the acts of God (Deut. 6). Indeed, in all those passages where the history of Israel with God is summarized in short reviews the starting point is always this encounter with the saving God. Encounter is a personal category. It dominates the whole of God's history with Israel.

This encounter occurred as an experience of saving. This is witnessed throughout the entire Old Testament in such depth and density that its significance is evident. In the Old Testament nothing of approximately equal significance can be placed side by side with it. The rescue from Egypt begins the history of the nation in the book of Exodus; on it is based the confederation of the tribes at the transition to the settlement (Josh. 24), and Deutero-Isaiah refers to it at the end of the history of the state with his promise of deliverance from the Babylonian exile.

The rescue from Egypt is related to worship in many ways: it is recited at the presentation of the first fruits (Deut. 26); one part of the salvation from Egypt is given as the reason for the Passover (Deut. 16); and finally, the exodus experience is recalled in the praise of God in liturgical Psalms (e. g., Ps. 136) as well as in the laments (e. g., Ps. 80; Isa. 63—64). God's saving act at the beginning of the history of Israel is regarded as the nucleus of the tradition, of the transmission to future generations (Deut. 6; Judg. 6:13). The commandments and laws are based on this event at the beginning, especially in the prologue of the Decalogue (Exod. 20; Deut. 5) and the deuteronomic paraenesis. The prophets refer to this event in particular as a contrast-motif in their historical reviews: e. g., Amos 2; 3; Jeremiah 2; Ezekiel 19; 20; and 23. Only the most important passages are mentioned here.[3]

All parts of the Old Testament (with the exception of the Wisdom literature) contain evidence for the lasting memory of the encounter with the saving God at the beginning. It has apparently permeated all areas of Israel's life. But it is not just a memory of the past, it has a very clear function for the present, as is evident in particular from the passages in the prophets and the Psalms.[4]

2. God Remains Israel's Savior

The experience of the rescue at the beginning means for Israel that Yahweh is going to *remain* Israel's savior. As he was the savior at the beginning, so his rescue continues to be expected, to be prayed for, and to be experienced. Yahweh is the saving God. This applies to the existence and history of the people as well as the existence and history of the individual. The historical books report further acts of saving and liberation. The rescue from Egypt is followed by many experiences of saving and preserving on the way through the wilderness, during the settlement, in the time of the Judges and (less frequently) of the kings, especially at the beginning of the latter: a king is granted to Israel for the purpose of rescue from the Philistine threat. The continuing experience of God's saving is most explicit in the communal laments, where the worshipers call to God for rescue from a present need by an express reference to his previous acts of salvation (as in Ps. 80 and Isa. 63—64).

During the exile Deutero-Isaiah promises liberation from the Babylonian captivity as a new exodus.

Indeed, this talking of God as the savior in present and future extends throughout the historical books, the prophets, and the Psalms.[5]

3. The Savior of Individuals, Humanity, and All Creatures

The reference to God as the savior is also applied to private life in the personal sphere. The majority of the Psalms of the individual tell of the saving acts of God: the cry out of need in the individual laments; the telling of experienced rescue from death in the individual narrative; Psalms of praise; the praise of the saving God "who looks into the depth" (Ps. 113, author's translation) in a group of descriptive Psalms of praise (hymns). But this experience of the saving God in the life of the individual is not related to the saving acts of God in the history of Israel (almost the only exception is Ps. 22). The experiences

of one's private life belong to a different sphere; the patriarchal narratives, for example, speak of saving actions of God in private life: in
the saving of the child dying of thirst (Gen. 21), in the jeopardy of
the ancestress in a foreign land (Gen. 12:10–20), in the saving of a
brother from his brother (Gen. 32) and of the youngest son in Genesis
37 and 44.[6]

There is a further expansion. In the Old Testament the saving acts
of God are not confined to his people and to the individuals in it. In
the primeval history and in apocalyptic, it is extended to all of humanity and to the animals. In the flood story (Gen. 6—9), God, who
destroys his creation, is at the same time the saving God, who in a
remnant preserves humanity and the animals from destruction.
Apocalyptic speaks similarly of destruction and saving (Isa. 24—27).
This is to say that the saving actions of God are unlimited; they occur
among the people of God, in the life of the individual, and for the
whole of humanity and the animals.

By speaking of God's saving in the spheres of national history, the
life of the individual, and of humanity and the whole creation, the Old
Testament indicates that God's saving has a far-reaching significance.
The experience of saving belongs to the whole of human existence. It
is something that everybody knows and which has occurred always
and everywhere throughout the history of humanity up to the present
day.

It is based on the fact that human beings are creatures. They are
created for life (as *naephaeš ḥajah*), but their life is limited. It follows
from the limitations of human life, as portrayed in Genesis 2—3, that
as long as humans live they are in danger, assailable, and vulnerable.
If they survive the danger, they know of the experience of being saved.
This applies to the individual, any human community, and to humanity as a whole. There is no human existence without danger. Being
saved is part of human existence.

Because the dangers and threats to human beings can be as varied
and can take on as many forms as human existence itself, the acts and
the experiences of saving can be very different indeed. This dis-
similarity does not alter the fact that God was, is, and shall be the
savior. The Old and New Testaments agree in this statement. The fact
that God is the savior is an aspect of his divinity in the Old as well

as in the New Testament. In the middle of the New Testament stands God's saving act in Christ; Christ is proclaimed as σωτήρ, and σωτηρία is a central term in the New Testament. It may seem that what is called saving in the book of Exodus and what is called saving in the New Testament have hardly anything in common; but first of all it is a fact that God is the savior both in the Old and in the New Testament. This conclusion needs no special exegesis; it stands quite independent of how one otherwise understands the relationship of the Old Testament to the New. This is a fact, which cannot be disputed: in the Old Testament as well as in the New the saving God has a central significance.[7]

B. The Act of Saving and History

1. The Elements of the Saving Act

The odd thing about the way the Old Testament speaks of the savior and the saving is that it does not emphasize the *state* caused by the saving, i. e., the "salvation" *(das Heil),* but rather the *process* of saving. Therefore the phrase "salvation history," if applied to the Old Testament, causes difficulties. The Old Testament does not narrate a history of salvation, but a history of the saving acts of God.[8]

The process of saving in the Old Testament occurs in a certain characteristic sequence of events. Saving can take place in many different ways and can be presented in very different forms; but the basic structure always remains the same: need—call out of need—hearing—saving—response of the saved persons. Two of these five elements are common to all talk of saving, especially to secular talk: the need and the turning away of need (saving).[9] The other three elements add the word to mere events: on the human side the call out of need and the response of the saved persons; on God's side the word of the savior, which, when he hears of the call out of need, precedes the saving intervention. These three elements turn the saving into an event in dialogue; by them the experience of saving from need becomes an encounter with the saving God, with which the history of Israel began.

This sequence or structure of events is shown by the "historic creed" in Deuteronomy 26:5–11[10] (author's translation):

The previous history	5: *"An Aramaean ready to perish was my father . . .*
Need	6: *"But the Egyptians oppressed us . . .*
Call from need	7a: *"Then we cried to Yahweh . . .*
Hearing	7b: *"And Yahweh heard us and saw our affliction . . .*
Saving	8: *"And Yahweh brought us out of Egypt . . .*
	9: *"and he brought us to this place and gave us this land.*
Response of the	10: *"And now I bring the first fruit . . . ."*
saved persons	11: *. . . you shall bow down and rejoice.*

This creed does not describe individual historic acts (as von Rad maintains), but a continuous process, whose individual elements form part of the whole.[11] The strength of the tradition of this creed is not based on an addition of individual events, but rather on the fact that so many and such diverse events from Egypt to Canaan have been melted into a single and confined arc of tension, which leads from need to saving.

2. The Composition of the Book of Exodus

The composition of the book of Exodus is based on the same structure, even if considerably extended. One such extension is already contained in the creed itself: the saving has been divided into two stages—the leading of the people *out* of Egypt and *into* Canaan, corresponding to the description of the saving in the book of Exodus. A second extension occurs in the section on "hearing." The hearing of the call out of need is bound up with the announcement of saving by a mediator, which bridges the wide gap between the oppression in Egypt and the arrival in the promised land. The scheme of promise and fulfillment is added to the history of God's act of saving, which is spread over a long period of time. In addition to this, many other expansions occur; nevertheless, in the composition of the book of Exodus the structure of the creed is clearly reflected.[12]

To the previous history, hinted at in Deuteronomy 26:5, corresponds "those who came to Egypt." (Exod. 1:1, author's translation)

The oppression in Egypt (Deut. 26:6) is described in detail in Exodus 1:6–22. The call from distress (Deut. 26:7*a*) is presupposed in Exodus 3:7, 9; the hearing (Deut. 26:7*b*) is connected with the promise of the exodus. Yahweh's leading of Israel out of Egypt (Deut. 26:8, 9) encompasses the books of Exodus, Leviticus, and Numbers. The response of the saved people is the psalm of praise Exodus 15.

The series of expansions has to be understood against the background of this basic structure and becomes meaningful in relation to it: Exodus 2—5 introduces the mediator (Moses), who brings the promise of saving to the Israelites oppressed in Egypt. The exodus is described in two stages: first, the liberation from a long-lasting oppression (connected with this are the miracles and plagues in Egypt, Exod. 7—11) and second, the saving from the threat of death, the Reed Sea miracle (Exod. 12—14). The leading of Israel into Canaan has been expanded along the way through the wilderness in Exodus 16—18 and Numbers 10—22 with new dangers and preservations.

Another expansion, which is no longer directly connected with the structure of saving, but which has been derived from it, is Exodus 32 —34, the breach and the renewal of the covenant. This expansion is based on the fact that those who have been saved deny their response to the savior. The denial of the response leads to apostasy, which has judgment as its consequence. The golden calf symbolizes the apostasy of the people to other gods, which becomes the great temptation after the settlement, as the accusation of the prophets (Elijah, Hosea) shows. Later traditionists are responsible for the fact that the apostasy of the people and the ensuing judgment immediately follow the deeds of God, which are the foundations of the history of the people.

But these elements, which form the history of the exodus from Egypt and the guidance into the land of Canaan, extend beyond this section of history and determine a large part of the Old Testament (as can be seen by the Deuteronomist's introduction to the book of Judges). The saving acts of God continue, God remains for Israel the saving God, as has been shown above. The announcement of saving forms the arc of tension from promise to fulfillment. The announcement of judgment is added to this whenever the savior is denied the proper response. The announcements of judgment and salvation govern prophecy. The event of which the book of Exodus speaks is an event in dialogue. The encounter begins with the call from distress; and the praise of those saved answers the savior. Praise and lament are the two main forms in the Psalms. The composition of the book of Exodus shares the basic actions of the three main parts of the canon.

C. Saving, Blessing, and Judging: The Old Testament Understanding of History

But certain sections of the Old Testament stand in no direct relation to the events of saving. The second part of the exodus promise: "I shall give you a land flowing with milk and honey" introduces a new stage of the history of Israel, which is no longer predominantly an act of saving as is the case on the way from Egypt to Canaan. It is the stage after the settlement and then after the formation of the state of Israel; it is determined in a stronger sense by the blessing than by the saving acts of God.[13] The transition occurs in Deuteronomy, where blessing is the dominant theological term. Kingship and worship after the settlement are determined essentially and predominantly by blessing; the legal corpora also belong to that time. The patriarchal history is to a large extent determined by blessing: it is the creator who blesses his creatures.

Blessing is to be the subject of the next part of this book, but I mention it now to correct the usual understanding of the working of God in the history of his people. For a long time this working of the God of Israel in history was regarded as the distinctive characteristic of Old Testament theology. This was seen in sharp contrast to the gods of the Near East, which were regarded as powers of nature, cosmic powers, whose working was determined by a cyclic understanding of time.[14]

Bertil Albrektson has objected to this because actions in history are also attributed to the gods of Israel's neighbors.[15] And James Barr has objected on the grounds that the Old Testament does not merely speak of God acting in history.[16] Both objections are justified. Von Rad, on the basis of his concept of salvation history, had worked from the presupposition that in the Old Testament the working of God in history consists of his deeds alone, that is to say, of acts in which he intervenes in history, saving or judging. He combined this with a purely linear interpretation of the Old Testament's understanding of time, so that time came to be regarded only as moving towards a target. Both can no longer be maintained in such a one-sided way. In the primeval history, time as motion towards a target is combined with time circling in the rhythms of creation, above all in Genesis 8:20–22: " 'While the earth remains, seedtime and harvest, cold and heat, summer and winter, day and night, shall not cease.' "[17] Cyclical and linear elements both always belong to the motion of time, even if time as motion towards a target has become more important for Israel. Time circling in the rhythms of creation remains; without it linear time would not exist.

For the other objection: in the Old Testament the working of God in history does not only consist of acts. The Old Testament knows at the same time of an equally important continuous working of God, which cannot be comprehended in individual acts and which is called blessing. The whole realm of nature belongs as much to the working of God as does the specific working in history.

So the specific character of the Old Testament understanding of history has to be defined afresh. We have found that the history from the exodus to the settlement is not depicted as a sequence of events but rather as a continuous happening, whose basic structure is the sequence of occurrences of saving as an event in dialogue (see above). We must now ask how this history continued.

Deuteronomy looks back and points to the danger that in the security of the settled existence the response can fail to occur, in other words to the danger of apostasy. The realization of this danger is indicated by the emergence and increase of the prophetic announcement of judgment. This forms a necessary contrast to the act of saving and its announcement in the exodus event. Even dwelling securely in the land and in secure cities under a king, Israel is again in danger. Only this time it is a different danger, a danger from inside, caused by turning away from Yahweh. The intention of the announcement of Yahweh's judgment over his own people is therefore—even if this seems paradoxical—similar to the announcement of saving at the beginning: Yahweh wants to turn away the deadly danger from his people. Thus the prophetic announcement of judgment, which occurs parallel with state and kingship, continues the history which had begun as a saving act of God to his people.

That this is really the case is apparent at the end of this period of history: the saving announced in the message of Deutero-Isaiah (and similarly in Ezekiel) after the judgment, i. e., after the political catastrophe, this saving from the Babylonian exile is tied to the announcement of saving from Egypt at the beginning but also to the prophecy of judgment. But the process of saving has now changed: now saving can only take place as a result of forgiveness (Isa. 40:1–11; 43:22–28). This can be shown by the structure of the process of saving: the announcement of forgiveness now appears together with God's hearing (the call from distress). Between the saving at the beginning and the saving from the Babylonian exile lies the period of history in which guilt had accumulated, which can only be eliminated by God himself by the announcement of forgiveness.[18]

Thus we have demonstrated a connection which led from the saving at the beginning by way of the announcement of judgment to the saving by forgiveness at the end. We can now draw the following conclusion: this very connection is special and unique to the history of Yahweh with his people Israel. This is only *one* line—a great deal more belongs to the history of God with his people—but it is the only line which shows the peculiar and unique character of the history of Israel and God.

D. Individual Elements and Examples

To develop this line fully we would have to present the individual elements of the process of saving in their own history: the call from distress (history of the lament in the Old Testament), the announcement of saving (history of the words of salvation in the Old Testament), the history of the mediator, and the history of the praise of God. To this we would have to add the narratives or reports of need and saving, i. e., the historiography in the Old Testament.

1. The History of the Mediator

We can sketch only two of these elements in a few lines. One part of the history of Yahweh with his people Israel is the history of the mediator. God's words and actions can be mediated to his people by a man. The mediator is no timeless figure; the working of the mediators can only be presented in a history. The patriarchal history does not yet know of the mediator; what is said and done between God and the patriarchs happens directly. The history of the mediator begins at the same time as the history of the people. Moses is mediator of God's words and actions. He mediates the announcement of saving, but he mediates also the exodus itself: he himself is the leader on the way through the wilderness. On the other hand, Moses is never the leader in battle.

After the settlement, the office of mediator is diversified: God frees his people by mediators of action, the so-called charismatic leaders, who are all leaders in battle, in wars of liberation but never of aggression. The kings are also mediators of saving to begin with; God gives them to his people to deliver them from the Philistine oppression. Saul marks the transition. After him, kingship develops a special royal theology which is determined by blessing (see below).

The mediators of action, that is to say men who mediate a liberating, saving act of God by being called and enabled by God to carry out the struggle of liberation, are confined to the short time between the settlement and the firm establishment of the monarchy. After this the office of mediator of action is discontinued. The important term of the *ruaḥ jhwh* is rooted in this time.[19] The prophets become the mediators of the word of God. But this has to be qualified. The prophets become mediators of the word of God in relation to history, which must be distinguished from the word of God in the context of worship, where the mediators are priests. To the Old Testament the mediator of the word is much more important than the mediator of action. The office of the mediator of the word has two stages: from the beginning of the monarchy it is reported in the books of Kings as an office in which the messenger had to announce God's salvation and judgment, but judgment only to the king. From the time of Amos onwards it is transmitted separately in the books of the prophets; from now on God's judgment is announced to the whole people. Although, within limits, the announcement of salvation remains, the announcement of judgment now becomes predominant.

And because the announcement is now predominantly one of judgment, it happens that the messenger of God, the prophet, can himself suffer under the execution of his message. This is most marked in the book of Jeremiah, where the suffering of the prophet finds expression in his laments (Jer. 10—20). This clearly approaches the office of Moses who as mediator of God's working for his people had to suffer as leader without power (the laments of Moses).

While in the case of Jeremiah the person and his fate become part of the office of messenger, it is in the Songs of the Suffering Servant in Deutero-Isaiah that, as in the beginning of history (Moses), the office of mediator is again an office which embraces word and "action" —here the suffering has taken the place of the action. His suffering on behalf of his people brings salvation to them. In this case it is most important that this office of mediator is no longer attested in the Old Testament itself as an integral part of the history of Israel, as were its predecessors. The poetic form of the Servant Songs leaves any relation to history open. If the New Testament says about Christ in all important points what the Servant Songs say about the Suffering Servant, then the whole history of the office of the mediator in the Old Testament could be represented by an incline, the goal of which is Christ, a goal which has been indicated by the Servant Songs.

2. Old Testament Historiography

The Old Testament historiography can only be touched on in a few points. The Pentateuch has as its nucleus the history of a saving. This saving was first of all sung in a short song of praise (Exod. 15:1–21), which from the beginning was combined with a short report of the event (Exod. 14). The praise of those saved became the nucleus of the Pentateuch, as has been shown with the "creed" in Deuteronomy 26.

As the Pentateuch is based on a confession of praise, so the Deuteronomistic History is based on a confession of sin. It arose out of the confession of guilt, which had to admit after the catastrophe that the prophetic accusation had been right.[20] The speeches that occur in various places throughout the entire Deuteronomistic History make it clear that the confession of guilt after the catastrophe is the nucleus of this work.[21]

Thus we have found a connection between the Pentateuch and the Deuteronomistic History which corresponds to the previous one: that in the Pentateuch the announcement of salvation (or promise) is dominant, in the time of the monarchy the announcement of judgment. The latter leads to the downfall, and the confession of guilt arises from the downfall. Here we have to emphasize again: this connection can only represent *one* prominent line of the fullness of the events described; this fullness ought not to be pressed into a pattern. This is impossible because of a further peculiarity of historiography in the Old Testament: it grows out of the description of individual events. We can still verify this because at the conception of the large works the traditionists have not destroyed the small units but preserved them, a multitude of speech-forms, which correspond to their respective contents.

In the process of tradition stretching over many centuries, there is a multitude of speech-forms, showing the working of God at various stages and in different forms of community. These are predominantly profane speech-forms: the family narratives in the patriarchal history; the sanctuary legends during the transition to settlement; the tribal sagas, hero sagas, and sagas about certain places during the time of the Judges; the multifarious stories of the wandering groups from the exodus out of Egypt until the arrival in the promised land; the narratives of promise; narratives about encounters with God; about alliances of the tribes and quarrels between them. After this follows the great caesura with the establishment of the monarchy and, simultaneously, the beginning of history writing, which produced the great works of the Yahwist and of the Succession Narrative and finally the great historical reviews of the time of the exile and the temple community, i. e., the Deuteronomistic and the Chronistic History Works.[22]

It follows from this that historiography in the Old Testament has two aspects: the one is the theological aspect discussed above, which gives the Old Testament its cohesion (confession of praise and confession of guilt); the other aspect consists of the fact that it is a grown and lively historiography, which developed out of each individual event, as it was experienced and transmitted by the individual in the small forms of narrative suited to it. In these forms historiography embraces all areas of life, which all share in the great theological contexts. In its nucleus it is neither a historico-political history, nor is it intended as a purely religious or "salvation" history; it is rather a history which includes human existence in all its areas and which receives its context and meaning from the relationship between God and man.

III
The Blessing God
and
Creation

A. The Creator and the Creation

The first sentence of the Bible implies that the Bible wishes to speak of the whole of being. When it speaks of the creator, it speaks of the universe. The creation narrative at the beginning of the Bible points to the horizon in which what it wants to say about God takes place. It is the whole world (Gen. 1) and the whole of humanity (Gen. 2), with which the God of the Bible deals. If both the Yahwist and the author of the Priestly Code begin their respective works, which aim at the history of Israel (J) and at worship in Israel (P), with creation and the primeval history, then they wish to express that the God of the people of Israel is not limited in his working by the boundaries of that people, but that he is the Lord of universal history and the Lord of the cosmos. Everything that happens between Israel and its God, everything that happens between an individual and God stands in this broad context.

1. The Primeval History (Genesis 1—11)

The first eleven chapters of the Bible speak of this broad context.[1] The creation of the world implies its possible destruction (Gen. 6—9); the creation of life entails its preservation by the power of reproduction and growth; the creator blesses his creatures. Blessing is effective in the series of generations in the depth of the dimension of time (Gen. 5) and in the breadth of the dimension of space across the breadth of the earth (Gen. 10).

The blessing of the creator is effective in the movement of the generations of the human race through time and through space; it is effective in the ever-constant rhythm of conception, birth, and death. With this rhythm of life the workings of the creator—the creator and the creation—reach into every generation, independent of all differences between people, of race, nation, or religion. As long as and wherever there is life, the creator is at work. At the creation, the creator acknowledges that "it was good." Because the word *tōb* means good *and* beautiful, beauty belongs to the creation and is reflected back in praise of the creator.

P expresses the special character of man among all manner of life by the clause that God created man in his image, to correspond to him (Gen. 1:26–27). This point is taken up again at the beginning of the fifth chapter, at the transition to the series of generations. God has created man in his image; that means in such a way that a relationship can exist between the creator and *this* creature, so that he may speak to him and he can answer him. This is peculiar to him among all creatures; thereby man has been given a dignity which only he possesses: human dignity. This has far-reaching consequences: all men possess this dignity throughout all generations (Gen. 5) throughout the earth (Gen. 10). It can be violated, desecrated, and ignored by people; but it cannot be destroyed by them. It has been conferred upon the human creature by the creator; as long as men exist, they are as God has created them in relation to him. Here the Bible makes a statement about man as God's creature independent of God's dealing with his elect people: human dignity is also attributed to those who do not belong to the people of God, the non-Israelites, the "heathen," the atheists. Human dignity belongs undeniably to all, even to the enemies of the faith.[2]

The blessing of the creator, in which he remains for all generations the creator, even includes death in the rhythm of his working. Without dying this rhythm would be impossible. Man has been created by God in an arc of existence from birth to death, and death at a ripe old age is no punishment, but rooted in the will of the creator, and, on the basis of this will, good and meaningful.[3]

But there are other deaths than peaceful; human life is endangered and vulnerable.[4] Therefore creation has its counterpart in the destruction threatening humans: the flood story corresponds to the creation narrative. People cannot really understand themselves as creatures if they are not conscious of the fact that the creator holds his creation in his hands in the face of all catastrophes which have happened and which are to come. Humanity has to live with catastrophes: no power in the world and no religion can alter this; but the promise of the creator at the end of the flood assures every generation that no catastrophe can cut off the creator's blessing. Even humans themselves with all their technical means cannot destroy their kind. Only God can put an end to humanity.

In the Yahwistic primeval history the creation of man stands in the foreground and therefore in the context of the danger which is inextricably bound up with the vulnerability of man on account of his own sin. Since humans are creatures, they can become guilty towards God (Gen. 3), and towards each other (Gen. 4), and they can be in danger of breaking through the limits which have been set for them (Gen. 3; 6:1–4; 11:1–9). Genesis 3 does not narrate a "fall," which is inherited by Adam's descendants, but rather it says about humans as God's creatures that they transgress God's command, which preserves them, and that this transgression separates them from God.[5]

2. The Creation of Man

The creation of man as described by the Yahwist expresses an understanding of humans as creatures that has been almost completely lost in Christian theology. Humans simply existing as separate individuals are not the creatures intended by God. To human existence belongs living-space (the garden), the provision of food (the trees of the garden), work (the commission to cultivate and preserve), and in particular the community (" 'a helper fit for him,' " Gen. 2:18).

This complex description of man's creation implies that people as God's creatures cannot be detached from their living-space, their provision of food, their work, or their community. They are only human *in* these relations, not beyond them in an abstract existence. A theological anthropology which wishes to describe man as such, without these relations, in relation to God alone, is not appropriate to man as God's creature. Were this to be recognized and accepted, it would have to cause a complete change in the way we talk about man in theology.

There exists a connection between this complex understanding of man's creation and the significance of blessing in the Old Testament. It is the working of the blessing that allows all these necessary parts of human existence to persist: God's blessing allows humanity's food to grow and prosper, preserves human living-space, gives people success in their work, and grants peace *(shalom)* within the community. A theology that is only soteriologically oriented is inclined to regard all these relationships as irrelevant and therefore to understand humanity as abstracted from them. But this is not in accordance with the Old Testament understanding. History as depicted in the Old Testament encompasses all areas of life, and humans are understood in their whole lifespan from birth till death, with everything that this life constitutes.

3. The Creation of the World

The same applies in a different way to the creation of the world.[6] In the Old Testament the entirety of the universe is primarily something which happens and only in a secondary sense something which exists. This has the consequence that if God is the creator of the world then everything that occurs in the world from the beginning to the end of time is in his hands. What began with the creation of heaven and earth must reach its destination: the history of the cosmos and the history of nature, the history of humanity and the history of his people. Therefore the Old Testament's speaking of the creator and the creation necessarily involves a universalism that attributes to the God whom Israel meets as her savior everything that happens from the beginning to the end of time. Thus in the Old Testament the end of time corresponds to the beginning of time; and apocalyptic, which speaks of a new heaven and a new earth, corresponds to the creation of heaven and earth. How deep the roots of this correspondence of beginning and end are is already apparent in the fact that in the structure of the primeval history (Gen. 1—11) creation and flood belong together. The flood has apocalyptic features, the promise at the end of the flood points to its limit: " 'While the earth remains . . . .' " It does not remain forever.[7]

This universalism, according to which all events are embraced by God, appears seldom in the Old Testament except in the primeval history and the apocalyptic; but it shines through again and again: when the beginning of the patriarchal history speaks of God's blessing for all generations of the earth, or when Psalm 148 calls all creatures in heaven and on earth to the praise of God. It is therefore not surprising that apart from the first chapters of the Bible the creator is spoken of in larger contexts in three places, which also intend to emphasize the universal aspect of the working of God: the first of these is the message of Deutero-Isaiah in which the breadth of God's working in creation is to give new confidence to the people who are despairing in Babylonian captivity: "The Lord, the eternal God who has created the ends of the earth, does not grow tired or weary" (Isa. 40:28, author's translation); further in the book of Job in which, in direct opposition to a narrow and rigid doctrine of retribution, the majestic greatness of the creator is at the same time the greatness of the one who shows pity to the sufferer; and finally the praise of God in the Psalms, praising God in the whole fullness of his godhead from the rising of the sun to its going down, from beginning to end.

B. The Blessing

In the creation account of the Priestly Code the creator blesses all manner of life: " 'Be fruitful and multiply . . . !' " (Gen. 1:28)[8] It is through this blessing that the creator works. The blessing is intended for all living beings; it is universal. As distinct from this, God's saving act is a special turning towards those who are being saved. Therefore a particular history arises out of the experience of saving: the history of those who have been saved, or salvation history. But those who have been saved remain human like everybody else and they are therefore in need of the blessing which embraces all people; they share in the gifts of the blessing, in their physical existence, in food and clothing, in the social and economic maintenance of the society in which they live, and in the continuation of life from one generation to the next. In the Old Testament all this is understood as the working of God by blessing, which encompasses all people and in which those who have been destined for a particular history with God also share.

1. The Distinctive Character of Blessing

Blessing is a working of God which is different from saving insofar as it is not experienced as the latter in individual events or in a sequence of events. It is a quiet, continuous, flowing and unnoticed working of God which cannot be captured in moments or dates. Blessing is realized in a gradual process, as in the process of growing, maturing, and fading. It is not as if the Old Testament is reporting only a series of events which consists of the great acts of God; the intervals are also part of it: in them God gives growth and prosperity unnoticed in a quiet working, in which he lets children be born and grow up, in which he gives success in work. The saving God is also the blessing God.

The meaning of this talk about blessing is that one can relate one's whole life, in its course from day to day and year to year, to God; one receives from God's hand one's whole life, especially in its daily unobtrusiveness, in which nothing particular happens. This is underlined by the fact that blessing and greeting are closely related and that the words "blessing" and "peace" are at the same time words of greeting.[9]

The flow of ordinary daily events usually takes place within the family. The two most important forms of community which determine human life, the nation and the family, are different in that in the history of the nation God's saving and judging are dominant, but in the family, the blessing. Therefore the patriarchal narratives are part of the Old Testament; they have something essential to say about man in relation to God and as a creature with all his needs and capabilities, in growing and maturing, in the increase and decline of his powers, in the course of everyday life and in the arc of existence from birth till death within the radius of a small circle of people which determines the course of the day and of life.

The Abraham cycle, which is concerned with the birth of a child, is introduced by a promise of blessing (Gen. 12:1–3); it is concerned with the threat to and preservation of the child, the mother, and the father. We are told that a child is preserved from thirst, that it is taken by God and returned, that the young man finds a wife and can begin a new generation, and that a family receives a future by their child.

The Jacob-Esau cycle deals with two brothers living side by side in a family, with the quarrel between these brothers and its consequences. In the Joseph story blessing is joined by peace *(shalom)* which originally means that the people within a community are at one with each other. We are told how the peace of a family was nearly destroyed and yet rehealed.[10]

What God does to the family in the patriarchal narratives, what the members of a family experience here looking up to God, belong inextricably to what the Bible says about God. Without this, he would not be the God of the Bible. The saving God is also the blessing God.

In the New Testament it is no different. The first two chapters of Luke's Gospel narrate events in the family; thus they correspond on purpose to the patriarchal history. The evangelist says that the working of God in blessing, as it finds expression in the context of the family, continues in the life and ministry of Jesus of Nazareth. If no child is born, no savior can come.[11]

2. Blessing Pertaining to Three Transitions

How God's blessing and saving belong together, but have to be distinguished, is shown in the three most important transitions of Israel's history.

a. The Transition into the *Kulturland*

To begin with, the transition from the way through the wilderness to the life in the *Kulturland.* The promise at the beginning of the exodus has two parts: it promises saving by the exodus from Egypt and the leading into "a beautiful, wide land, flowing with milk and honey." This is the language of blessing which describes the beauty and abundance of the promised land. It is a blessed country, into which God wants to lead them. When Israel has arrived in the land and has adopted the habits of settled life, then blessing will acquire a great significance for it.[12] On the way through the wilderness and during the exodus from Egypt the people were totally dependent on God's saving and keeping; the way was a continuous, steep up-and-down of need and rescue. With the settlement, the people became dependent on the rhythms of life of the *Kulturland,* seed and harvest, growth and prospering, and therefore on the blessing of God. This change is indicated by the structure of the Pentateuch: the complex Exodus through Numbers, which is totally determined by God's saving acts, is followed by Deuteronomy. In the speech of Moses at the threshold of transition into the *Kulturland,* the term "blessing" is dominant;[13] and the promise of blessing is renewed before the entry into the land (Deut. 7:13–16, author's translation; similarly 28:3–6):

He shall love you and increase you and bless you.
He shall bless the fruit of your body and the fruit of your ground,
your grain, your must and your oil,
the increase of your cattle and the young of your flock
within the land that the Lord swore to your fathers to give you.

The traditionists were fully aware that there was a change in the way Israel talked about God's working with the transition to settled life. This is stated in a short note at the beginning of the book of Joshua: "And the manna ceased . . . when they ate of the produce of the land; and the people of Israel had manna no more, but ate of the fruit of the land of Canaan." (Josh. 5:12) The bread of blessing now takes the place of the bread of saving.

This transition involved one of the most difficult internal arguments in the history of Israel, in which the belief in the *one* Yahweh prevailed, who also has to be acknowledged and venerated as the giver of the blessing. The radical struggle against the Baal religion in Deuteronomy and in the prophets, especially Hosea, is directed against the Baal religion as a fertility religion. This has largely led in Old Testament interpretation and theology to a wrong conclusion: that Yahweh the God of Israel is only the God of history, and that "nature-religion" and the "fertility-cult" would be radically rejected in Yahweh religion. But that is not the case. For Hosea, who led the most intense struggle against the Baal religion, Yahweh the God of Israel is also the God who blesses. In chapter 2 he confronts the Baalim not with the God of history, but with the God who blesses and gives fertility and prospering. " 'And she did not know that it was I who gave her the grain, the wine, and the oil.' " (Hos. 2:8) Hosea wishes to say by this that Yahweh the God of Israel, whom Israel meets as savior in its history, is the *same* God who gives Israel in the *Kulturland* the gifts of the land, growth, and prospering. This does not make the religion of Israel a fertility religion; but the God of Israel as the blessing God gives his people the same gifts that in other religions are expected from the fertility gods. The first commandment has to be understood against the background of this struggle.

With the transition to settled life comes the adoption of the form of worship that corresponds to this life-style, together with the previously Canaanite sanctuaries of the country. God's work of blessing, the gift of grain, wine, and oil (Hos. 2:8; Deut. 7:13), is celebrated in the agricultural festivals which Israel inherited from the settled people. Even after they have been "historicized" in Israel, i. e., even after they have been connected with the acts of God in history, they still remain festivals in the course of the year, which celebrate seed and harvest (e. g., Ps. 62). The life of the farmer who depends on the blessing of fertility passes in the natural rhythms of the year which find expression in the religious festivals.[14]

The liturgical blessing, given during worship at the holy place and at the holy time, only acquired significance for Israel after the settlement. The priestly blessing (Num. 6:22–27) is given at the end of every sacrificial act of worship (Lev. 9:22–23); the visitors to the festivals and the services, and the pilgrims in the processions (Ps. 24) receive from the sanctuary the blessing for their house, their family, and their work. The Psalms demonstrate the significance of this blessing: the priests bless the congregation (Pss. 115:14–15; 118:26; 129:7–8; 134:3) or an individual (Pss. 91; 121). At the procession the blessing is given from the sanctuary (Pss. 24:5; 118:26; 128:5). The whole country, the houses and fields, families and cattle, expected and received the blessing of fertility, which meant growth and prospering. At the presentation of the sacrifices, in particular the first fruits, the received blessing was acknowledged as God's gift; this flow of blessing to and from the sanctuary was an essential part of the life of the Israelite farmer. The liturgical institution of the blessing is concerned with nothing other than the working of God in blessing, of which Deuteronomy speaks, and likewise the patriarchal narratives with their promise of blessing, the Balaam story (Num. 22—24), and many other texts.[15]

In addition to this, the basic elements of worship after the settlement—the holy place, the holy time, the holy act, led by a mediator (priest), with its regular character, with the regular rhythms of the annual festivals—all these elements point to the continuous working of God and to the rhythm of his working in blessing, as it is established at the end of the flood in Genesis 8:22: " 'While the earth remains . . . .' "[16]

How Israel combined the memory of God's acts in its history and the celebration of these with the established form of regular worship, is brought out particularly by the sacrificial saying in Deuteronomy 26, where "the historic creed" occurs in the context of the presentation of the first fruits: the savior of Israel has become the giver of the blessing, the gifts of the land are received from his hand.

b. The Transition to Kingship

At the second transition, the transition to kingship, a change is manifested in the role of the mediator. The charismatic leaders, the so-called Judges, were savior-figures, mediators of the saving working of God for his people. Initially this role was also intended for kings: they were to be saviors from Philistine oppression. But kingship had its own theology which eventually prevailed. This theology is based on the idea that the king represents the power of the state, in the dynastic form together with his family, and that this power is confirmed by God. The promise to David through Nathan (2 Sam. 7) differs strongly from the old promises; the king and his house are promised continuity. Kingship in Israel has features which are peculiar to it and which have been formed from specifically Israelite tradition, but besides this it has features which it shares with kingship outside Israel. All kingship is sacral, even if the sacral character can find quite different expression. It is one of the essential functions peculiar to sacral kingship that the king is mediator of blessing: the king is responsible for the well-being and prospering of his people and country, he therefore also has liturgical functions and can give the blessing on special occasions (1 Kings 8).[17] Thus there is a difference between these two types of mediators of the word of God: the priest is primarily a mediator of God's blessing; the prophet a mediator of God's judging and saving.

c. The Transition Caused by the Collapse of the State

At the third transition, caused by the collapse of the monarchy and the state, blessing in many different contexts determines the expectation of the future.

There is no mention of the blessing, or hardly any, in those parts of the Old Testament that speak in a very concentrated way of God's saving (Exodus through Numbers) or judgment (prophecy of judgment). But they are looking across into a future determined by blessing. The beginning of the exodus (Exod. 3:7–8) and the end of the wilderness wandering (the blessings of the seer Balaam, Num. 22—24) both look forward to the beauty and richness of the promised land (everywhere in the Old Testament blessing is connected with beauty).[18] Similarly, the prophecy of judgment also looks beyond the arrival of judgment into a changed future. This change—both in form and content—points again to a distinction between God's saving and blessing.[19]

First, the distinction in form: the announcement of judgment corresponds to the announcement of salvation—both announce an event. Isaiah for instance announces in chapter 7 that Jerusalem shall not fall into the hands of the approaching enemies. On the other hand, the description of blessing depicts a condition in an undetermined future, which will be opposed to the present one. The Old Testament contains many such descriptions of salvation or blessing; they increase in frequency in later times, approximately from the exile onwards. For instance the "messianic prophecies" speak of the realm of peace of a king of salvation. Wars will cease (Isa. 9; 11; 26:12); growth and prospering will be unlimited (Zech. 9:17; Isa. 65:16b–25; 66:11); all shall be happy and content (Micah 4); there shall also be peace among the animals (Isa. 11; 65:25). This shows to what extent Israel saw the king as the mediator of blessing; above all, it is significant that the king of the realm of peace never becomes king by defeating his enemies in war—on the contrary, he is born the king of peace (Isa. 9).

Second, the change in content: the promise of saving changes with the collapse of the state and the monarchy. The message of Deutero-Isaiah no longer proclaims the restoration of the state and the sovereignty; the mediator of saving in Deutero-Isaiah is a heathen king, the saving from exile is no longer Israel's victory. The promise of blessing has now been combined with the promise of Israel's return to her country; in the middle of chapters 54—55 stand growth, increase, and flourishing in the land received by Israel again.[20] Similarly, Trito-Isaiah no longer announces an event of saving, but a change of the conditions.

In a different way in Jeremiah the promise of blessing takes the place of the announcement of saving. In the promise connected with the purchase of the field at Anathoth shortly before the fall of Jerusalem, Jeremiah says nothing of the saving of the besieged city of Jerusalem, and has only the very minimum to say about what will happen after the destruction: life shall continue in the city: " 'Houses and fields and vineyards shall again be bought in this land.' " (32:15) In his letter to the exiles (29:4–7), Jeremiah only sees a future for them in the line of blessing. God's working in blessing his people continues even after the collapse of the state and the monarchy.

For apocalyptic the description of blessing is the typical way of talking about future salvation. In it the announcement is absent completely; apocalyptic can only speak of salvation in the future in a timeless depiction, where it looks beyond the apocalyptic catastrophe. This depiction of blessing is universal; with the end of history, the differentiation into nations is dropped, and God acts as in the primeval history with the whole of humanity. As the creator blessed man and animals, so in the eschaton man and animals share in the universal peace.

3. The Problem of Blessing in the Book of Job

The most urgent theological problem after the exile was a question, not about the saving, but about the blessing God. Part of the

Wisdom literature, some of the Psalms (especially Ps. 73), and the whole of Job circle around this question. The question was: how is it possible that so many godless people participate in blessing and so many God-fearing people have to suffer and do not prosper? Two quite different answers have been given. One is the answer of Job's friends: God blesses only the God-fearing; and if there is hard suffering and a lack of blessing, the sufferer must have sinned gravely. The other answer is given by the writer of Job: Job cannot believe his friends. He clings to the God who smites him. He cannot understand God, but he clings even in rebelling against God. This, in the personal sphere of life, corresponds to the Servant of the Lord in the history of the people. Both suffer without the meaning of their suffering being apparent, and both are waiting for a new word from God: the Yes to the suffering, the Yes to the sufferer. Death can no longer be the end of God's blessing.

4. Parallels from Other Religions

From all this arises a final distinction between God's working in saving and blessing. We have found that the Old Testament talks of blessing in particular in the life of the family, in the agriculture of the settled life, in the form of worship after the settlement, and in connection with kingship. All these are areas in which a connection with non-Israelite religions is not only possible but in fact attested in the Old Testament.[21] It is due to the universal character of the blessing that agreements with other religions occur more readily in connection with God's working in blessing rather than with his working in saving, which introduces a particular and unique history. In the patriarchal history the God who deals with Abraham, Isaac, and Jacob is the "God of Abraham" or God of the Fathers; only at a later stage was this God identified with Yahweh, the God of Israel. In the circle of family life, the working of the blessing God reaches back, according to the Old Testament's own statement, into the time before Israel's encounter with Yahweh. The community-form of the family belongs to pre-political life, it precedes the division of humanity into nations and religions. The elementary processes of life are the same in the whole world, revolving around birth, marriage, and death, subsistence and security of life.[22] Blessing as the divine power of fertility is one of the oldest and most widespread motifs in the religions of all peoples. Everywhere that growth and prospering are expected from a divine power, this expectation is expressed in liturgical forms, which are connected with seed and harvest, above all the annual festivals. Therefore, in the religions of many settled societies, worship has the same basic features as can be found in the worship of Israel. A place of worship stands in the middle of a settlement, and families and individuals come to it at regular times for communal acts of worship, led by a mediator (priest). One of these communal acts is the sacrifice, which is common to very many religions. When the Israelites during their immigration took over Canaanite sanctuaries they also took over with them certain basic features of liturgical tradition, even if the worship of Israel was fundamentally new. We know this in particular from the worship in Jerusalem. Kingship in the Old Testament itself is depicted as something which has been taken over from other peoples, and therefore it is only natural that it contains, besides specifically Israelite features, many features common to kingship in general. Consequently, for many Old Testament texts dealing with kings or kingship, a multitude of extra-Biblical parallels can be found.

In conclusion, we may say that God's working in blessing has obvious connections with similar elements in other religions: in the gift of the threefold blessing of fertility, in the structure of worship after the settlement, and in God's working in the family and in kingship. In all these areas, parallels in other religions can be found. The same applies to the working of God as the creator, and to the primeval history as a whole.

God's saving cannot be separated from his blessing; both are constantly interlocked and combined with each other. So both receive their due: the singularity and uniqueness of the history of God with his people in the one aspect of God's working, the agreement with the other religions in the other.

IV
God's Judgment and God's Mercy

A. Sin and Judgment: The Prophets of Doom

When the Bible mentions the fact that God punishes or acts as a judge, this seems to contradict what the Bible says about God otherwise: God created men—so why didn't he just create them in such a way that he would never need to punish them? God blesses people; he saves those threatened by death—so why does he destroy his saving and blessing again and again by punishments?

1. Sin as a Human Phenomenon

This latter question points to an insurmountable limitation of man in deed as well as in thought. It is simply a human limitation that people transgress, that they sin. Thus they can only speak of God by including judgment and punishment. This contradiction cannot be solved; it is part of human existence. Therefore sin, human transgression and God's intervention against it, is already part of the primeval history; this indicates that this human transgression which we call sin is characteristic of human beings: no religion and no structure of society can change the fact that people of all times, all races, and all ideologies transgress by nature. When, then, in the primeval history human sin is each time followed by God's intervention, this is motivated by the hindering, disturbing, and destructive effect of sin. An Egyptian text once called human sin "the great disturbance." By sin something or somebody is always endangered, whether this becomes immediately apparent or remains hidden for a long time.

It is the intention of the Yahwist in his narratives of guilt and punishment in Genesis 1—11 to depict human transgression in its many varied possibilities in order to make clear the impending danger to man in these possibilities: the transgression of the individual against the creator in an act of disobedience which threatens the relationship of trust between God and man (Gen. 3), fratricide (Gen. 4), and the despising of a father (Gen. 9:20–27).[1]

To this has to be added the possibility of collective sin in the crossing of the border into the superhuman (Gen. 6:1–4; 11:1–9) and the corruption of a whole generation (Gen. 6—9). In all these stories the narrator of the primeval history describes sin as a universal phenomenon. At the same time the writer points out an important distinction in the reaction of God the creator to human transgressions. On the one hand God intervenes as judge, especially in Genesis 3 and 4, where this judicial intervention corresponds precisely to the profane trial, which can be found universally in the institution of courts (discovery of the crime—hearing—defense—sentence). It is God the creator who in the worldwide institution of the independent court opposes the transgressor and restricts evil. On the other hand the flood story shows a different reaction of God to human transgression: the flood is an act of God's judgment for the hybris of a whole generation which has grown beyond all limits (Gen. 6:5*a*, 7*a*, J). But at the end of the flood the creator declares solemnly that such a destruction shall never occur again: " 'I will never again curse the ground because of man, for the imagination of man's heart is evil from his youth.' " (Gen. 8:21) In this decision at the end of the flood the creator promises the preservation of the world in spite of all human inclination to evil. God wishes to preserve and keep humanity as it is. His reaction to the human inclination to evil is patient suffering; it is not the reaction of the judge. Jesus says likewise: " 'for he makes his sun rise on the evil and on the good, and sends rain on the just and on the unjust.' " (Matt. 5:45)

2. Sin in the History of God's People

From sin as a human phenomenon, human transgression which is part of human existence, we have to distinguish the sin of the people of God and its individual members in the mutual relationship of Israel to her God. This sin only becomes possible through the encounter of Israel with Yahweh; it is a process in the history of Israel with her God. Every possible transgression, every possible sin has already been preceded by something, namely Israel's experiences with God, the experience of the acts of saving and the receipt of his gifts.[2] It is sufficient to point out one word which makes this connection clear: the word "forget." It is often used by Jeremiah in his accusation. The transgressions of the people of Israel which lead to his accusation are rooted in this act of forgetting: only because the present generation has forgotten God's deeds and gifts for Israel could such transgressions arise.

These transgressions of Israel can only be understood in close connection with her history; they are themselves a historical phenomenon and as such subject to change (in contrast to the concept of sin in the Western Christian tradition—in which sin has become an unhistorical timeless phenomenon). The unique characteristic of the history of Israel, as described in the Old Testament, consists of the very fact that the sin of Israel towards her God has been taken so very seriously that it decisively determined the history. Israel's sin begins when Israel itself begins: the exodus from Egypt contains the event of the golden calf (Exod. 32—34). Israel's history with God is like an incline: the guilt of Israel before God grows to such an extent that it leads to his intervention against his own people in judgment. This is the very nucleus of the message of the prophets of judgment: the announcement that God will punish or even destroy his own people, based on an accusation.[3]

Remember that Israel's sin is not something which exists of necessity; Israel is *not* by its very nature a sinful people. On the contrary, at the beginning a good and intact relationship between God and his people is presupposed. This is the meaning of the frequently used image of marriage. In Deuteronomy, remaining in the promised land and the continuation of the blessing are made dependent on the obedience of the people; it is presupposed that this condition can be fulfilled and that therefore the relationship between God and his people can remain intact. Similarly in the review of the Deuteronomistic History the idolatry of the kings of Israel and Judah, which causes God's judgment, is not general: David and a few other kings are exempt.

It is not only in prophecy that the guilt of Israel in the context of its history is seen. The Deuteronomistic History also shows this incline which led to the catastrophe.[4] The clearest sign of this incline is the fact that the prophets of judgment before Amos have voiced *no* accusation against Israel as a whole nation. Therefore the accusation against the whole nation has an added stress. It is voiced from the time of Amos up till Jeremiah and Ezekiel, and it gives the reason for the announcement of catastrophe.

3. The Prophecy of Judgment

There has been a phenomenon like prophecy—taken in a very broad sense—in many religions. There has even been a form of prophecy that shows similarity in its very wording to the prophecy of Israel: the prophecy of Mari by the Euphrates. But only in Israel has there been this succession of prophets from Amos to Jeremiah and Ezekiel, who through this long period of time have steadfastly announced the intervention of a god against his own people in judgment. The prophecy of judgment has to be seen in close connection with the beginnings of Israel: with the saving from Egypt and the guidance through the wilderness, which only then made Israel a people. Israel obtained its very existence as a nation by God's acts of saving; if Israel forgot God, if it turned against this God and away from him, then it would thereby lose the basis of its existence.[5] This is the reason for the appearance of the prophets. Their accusations and announcements of judgment were concerned with Israel's existence. Thus the saving God is now the judging God; the judgment announced by the prophets is the necessary continuation of the saving working of God. This judgment is aimed, paradoxically, at the saving of Israel—through and after the judgment. God's acts in saving and judging his people belong closely together.

We can illustrate this point even more clearly. The prophetic accusation is not concerned with individual sins nor with the fact that

Israel is a sinner in a general and abstract way; it is concerned rather in each case with transgressions which put the existence of Israel as the people of God in danger. The Old Testament knows no abstract and timeless concept of sin, which would be similar to a concept of being. Sins and transgressions are only mentioned when they threaten human existence, the human community, or the community between God and man. This threat is never the same; it is derived from the historic, economic, cultural, and religious circumstances; consequently it changes.[6]

This historic character of sin is clearly manifest in the prophetic accusation. It is not always the same, it changes from one prophet to another and also within the same prophet from one period of his ministry to another. The accusations of the prophets before Amos were mostly directed towards a king; they have to be understood against the background of the historical situation, just as the prophetic tradition afterwards is still a part of the historical tradition. Nathan's accusation against David and Elijah's against Ahab have their respective meanings only in the situation in which a threat to Israel arises from the behavior of the king; and it is against this that the accusation is directed. Thus the emphasis of the accusation changes from one prophet to another and we obtain from them a surprisingly accurate reflection of the cultural, social, economic, political, and religious events of their respective times. Sometimes the emphasis is on social accusation (especially Amos and Micah), sometimes on idolatry (Hosea and Ezekiel), on political accusation combined with an attack on hybris (Isaiah), on the deserting and forgetting of Yahweh (Jeremiah), or on worship which has become insincere (Amos, Jeremiah). These are only examples; they show the surprising liveliness of the prophetic accusation. The prophets are never interested in compiling catalogues of vices to demonstrate to their contemporaries what kind of bad people they are; on the contrary, they point to the respective crises, i. e., where the threat lies in the present hour.

But this is only possible when the prophets pit their whole existence on their commission: to announce God's judgment on the basis of these accusations of Israel. The prophets' total identification of themselves with their office is a characteristic of prophecy in Israel.

This has two sides: one of them is manifest in the language of the prophets. Each speaks his own language and introduces into this language the tradition in which he has grown up, so that we can recognize more or less clearly his *"geistige Heimat"* (intellectual and spiritual home, Hans Walter Wolff). It is in most cases a profane language, differing strongly from the language of a priestly-sacral school; it is the language of a living man, whose personal fate, whose thoughts and emotions, whose involvement in the message which he has to pass on, all form part of this language. The prophets as mediators of the word of God are men of their time; while in the very midst of experiencing the present, they are under commission to accuse and to announce judgment on it. They themselves are sitting in the boat whose capsizing they have to announce. The other side has thus already been hinted at: the commission brings them no reward or honor, but it can certainly bring them suffering. From the history of Israel's apostasy springs the history of the suffering of those individuals who in their message oppose this apostasy: the suffering of the mediator. How the suffering of the mediator forms part of the new context of God's mercy beyond judgment, we shall discuss in the following.

B. God's Compassion and the Prophecy of Salvation

1. The "Inconsequence of God" and the Prophets

In its talk about God, the Old Testament contains a very peculiar feature which makes God's actions at a certain point appear very human. As opposed to other contexts, which emphasize the holiness of God in contrast to man, here a human emotion is attributed to God: the emotion of compassion. The Hebrew word for this, *rhm* (or its plural), actually means "mother's womb"; or the compassion of the father for his child (Ps. 103) can become the image of this divine compassion.[7] It is very often connected with an "inconsequence of God"; i. e., this divine compassion frequently occurs where a totally different reaction of God would be appropriate. This is why this divine compassion appears so human. In the narratives of guilt and punishment in Genesis 1—11, God's reaction to the human guilt never ends simply with the punishment. Somehow he always moderates the punishment; e. g., at the expulsion from the garden, God makes skirts from skins for the man and his wife, so they need not be ashamed. This divine compassion acquires the most decisive significance after the occurrence of the divine judgment by the destruction of the state, the kingship, and the temple. The "inconsequence" of God which is connected with his compassion is most apparent at this point in the entire history of Israel: the destruction has been announced by the long sequence of prophets of judgment—but in spite of this a turning occurs for the remnant.

As the prophets had been the messengers of God's judgment, so once again the prophets were the messengers of this turning. The prophets were never messengers of doom alone. At certain times the prophets of judgment have spoken oracles of salvation too, especially Isaiah, e. g., in chapter 7. These messages of compassion are special, however, and are always connected with the prophet's message of judgment. This can be particularly recognized in Hosea and Jeremiah. The language of compassion is connected immediately with the announcement of judgment in Hosea 11:8–9: "How can I give you up, O Ephraim! How can I hand you over, O Israel! . . . My heart recoils within me, my compassion grows warm and tender." Here too the same inconsequence: compassion breaks through in spite of the announcement of judgment. In Jeremiah, we find something similar in the peculiar motif of God's lament which is connected with the announcement of judgment, e. g., Jeremiah 9:10–12, 17–22. God suffers under the judgment that he has to bring upon his people.

We have to point to a further connection: in the visions of Amos (7:1–9; 8:1–3; 9:1–6) the prophet as intercessor begs for the compassion of God upon the people's need, and in the first two visions (7:1–3, 4–6) this is granted. In the three subsequent visions, however, this compassion is denied: " 'I will never again pass by them!' " (7:8; 8:2; 9:4) The announcement of judgment takes the place of God's turning towards Israel in compassion. God can now no longer show compassion, he can no longer forgive his people. Still, God's compassion is not extirpated, it is only withheld, until it breaks through again after the judgment. This is the very message of Ezekiel and Deutero-Isaiah: after judgment, there can be a message of comfort (Isa. 40:1–11). As in the visions of Amos, the lament of the people in need is presupposed; it is the many-sided lament after the catastrophe (e. g., Isa. 40:27), to which the message of the prophet in the form of the oracle of salvation comes as the divine answer. And it is, once again (as in the first two visions of Amos), the answer of divine compassion (Isa. 40:28–31; 41:8–16; 43:1–7).

2. God's Mercy and Forgiveness

But in this new compassionate turning of God towards his people, which brings the time of judgment to an end, a difference has to be noted in comparison with former demonstrations of God's compassion. Compassion is only possible in connection with God's forgiveness. The forgiveness of the guilt which had accumulated during the time of the announcement of judgment has to be explicitly stated and has to be pronounced immediately to the people of God. Compassion without forgiveness would have no meaning in this situation—it could not bring about a real change. There can only be a change when the relationship between God and his people becomes intact again, and this is only possible through forgiveness. Therefore Deutero-Isaiah's message of comfort has as its very first words an announcement of forgiveness: "cry to her that her time of service is ended, that her iniquity is pardoned!" (Isa. 40:2) The complete agreement of the two exilic prophets in this is important. Ezekiel also assumes that the restoration of the people (Ezek. 37) will be combined with a cleansing of the people from their sins (Ezek. 36:16–38).

With this we have to compare what has been said about God's compassion to his people at the beginning of the history of Israel, at the beginning of the book of Exodus: " 'I have seen the affliction of my people who are in Egypt, and have heard their cry because of their taskmasters; I know their sufferings.' " (Exod. 3:7) In this case it is God's pure compassion with these sufferers: "I know their sufferings"; this turning is brought about simply by the saving out of need, need caused by suffering. In this case no history has yet taken place and no guilt has accumulated; God's compassion is simply the compassion towards the suffering creature, in the same way as his compassion turns towards the child dying of thirst in Genesis 21:17.

It is on the basis of this compassion for the sufferer that the promise on its way through the Old Testament must be understood, beginning with the promises to the patriarchs, taken up by the prophets of salvation, and ending with the promises in the context of apocalyptic. The way of the promise through the Old Testament is the strongest expression of continuity in the history of the people of God; it holds together large epochs—for example, the promises to the patriarchs bind that period with the period of the people in Canaan.[8]

Both therefore have their place, their meaning and their necessity: God's compassion which turns towards the suffering creature and God's compassion on the basis of forgiveness which heals a broken community. It is of great significance for the Old Testament's talking about God that both are mentioned. Both are part of God's mercy: the compassion towards the sufferer and the compassion towards the sinner.

3. God's Compassion on an Individual: Sin and Forgiveness in Different Contexts

We have so far spoken only of God's compassion towards the people. A large number of texts attest God's compassion towards an individual. But whereas God's compassion towards his people is nearly always confined to the prophetic message, talk about God's compassion towards an individual has its place in the language of prayer: in the pleading for compassion in the individual laments and in the praise of God which looks back to the hearing of this pleading, or which praises God's compassion in summary form.[9] But the circle of God's compassion has to be drawn even larger: even the suffering animal is included; when God desists from his judgment on the city of Nineveh, his compassion includes the little children and the animals (Jonah 4:11). God's compassion is effective in all acts of forgiveness, but the Old Testament talks about sin and forgiveness in different contexts.[10]

a. The God of the Family

The Old Testament does not speak of sin and forgiveness everywhere; such talk is absent particularly in the patriarchal history (in Gen. 12—36). In this case, a relationship between the patriarchs and their God is depicted in which there is no mention of sin against God and God's forgiveness. The reason is probably that the "God of the Fathers," as the God of a family who lead a nomadic life in a constantly threatened existence, is completely a God *for* this small group and this group is completely dependent on him.[11] In many Psalms of the individual, especially in the motif of trust, this entirely personal relationship with God lives on.

b. The Joseph Story

In the Joseph story, guilt and punishment is a motif which propels the narrative; but this happens in a community between people—not, or only very much in the background, between people and God. But the story does say something essential for the understanding of guilt and forgiveness in the Old Testament. It shows that sin and guilt can only arise where something happens between people. When someone becomes guilty, the *shalom,* the intactness of the community, is broken. This is shown in the suffering of at least one member of this community; sin or guilt in a community always causes suffering, abstract sin does not exist. This understanding of guilt, according to which it is a process in the community, differs fundamentally from an individualistic-abstract understanding of sin, where the entire emphasis lies on the individual's consciousness of sin. But the Joseph story shows something essential for forgiveness also: forgiveness has its time. It does not occur automatically (guilt—confession—forgiveness), but is so woven into the history of the individual and the community that the hour eventually comes when the admission of guilt and thereby the forgiveness become possible. This corresponds to the forgiveness which is announced to Israel; it too has its time, and here also the admission of guilt has come only after a long process.

c. Forgiving in Worship

The act of forgiving in worship is completely different. In this case, an act of forgiveness, which is by its very nature a personal one, has become institutionalized, and it is pronounced by the cult-mediator, the priest. The act of atonement, connected with sacrifice, takes the place of the immediate pronouncement of forgiveness. The confession of sin (Lev. 5:5) is joined by the act of penance (Lev. 5:6), consisting of the presentation of a sacrificial animal. In postexilic times we find a big increase of the sacrifice of atonement;[12] some kinds of sacrifices, which previously had a different function, now become sacrifices of atonement. After the exile a special liturgy was introduced for the atonement of the sins of the people: the great Day of Atonement (Lev. 16). The ritual of atonement was obviously of very great significance in the later days of Israel. It is significant that the ritual of atonement has become completely divorced from history, and that the atonement of guilt is no longer possible without the cultic institution and the priest.

d. Forgiveness in the Servant Songs

What is said about forgiveness in the Songs of the Suffering Servant (Isa. 42:1–4; 49:1–6; 50:4–9; 52:13—53:12) stands in strong contrast to this. It is closely connected with the history of the people of God and can only be understood in this context. For a clarification of the work of the Suffering Servant in the Songs, we must look to Isaiah 43:22–28.[13] In this passage, Deutero-Isaiah speaks of the mountain of guilt which had accumulated in the history of Israel, and which could not be erased by the sacrifices: "you have burdened me with your sins [or: you have made me serve]." Israel's sin is a burden; the removal of it requires service. And for the person of the Suffering Servant, we have to refer to the laments of the prophet Jeremiah (Jer. 10—20): the ministry of the prophets—especially Jeremiah—has led to their suffering; Isaiah 49:4 alludes to the suffering of the prophet: "But I said, 'I have labored in vain, I have spent my strength for nothing and vanity.' " The ministry of the prophets which appeared to be a failure is taken up in the work of the Suffering Servant and now receives its meaning in the suffering of the Servant as a deputy: "for our iniquities" (Isa. 53:5), "stricken for the transgression of my people." In the final section of the last Song of the Suffering Servant, two lines of the Old Testament's talk about God converge. First, it is reported that the suffering of the Servant does not end in the abyss of death. God shows pity on the sufferer and responds to the sufferer's lament, as he showed pity on the laments of Jeremiah and on the laments of the many nameless sufferers in the Psalms of lament. In this compassion towards the sufferer, something else happens: this one has suffered in the service of God, has suffered as God's Servant and as a deputy for the sins of the people. He is a Servant in the sequence of the servants of God, his suffering is the suffering and death of the mediator. This other aspect brings the line of the mediator in the Old Testament to an end: in the ministry of the Suffering Servant, the ministry of all the mediators throughout the Old Testament reaches its destination. But the Servant is only spoken of in a veiled manner and by hints; he does not have a name: only outside the Old Testament is he given a name. Even then, it will be God's compassion turning to human suffering, which sends the mediator: "For God so loved the world. . . ."

V

The Response

One side of what takes place between God and humanity is response. Contrary to the opinion that prayer and offering are works initiated by humans, both are understood in the Old Testament as response; there would be neither cult nor prayer if it were not for the acts and words of God. Corresponding to this, it must also be said that the acts and words of God cannot remain unanswered. God acts and speaks in order to elicit a response. What happens in the Old Testament between God and humanity has the form of a dialogue.[1]

A. The Response in Words

1. The Praise of God

The very first chapter of the Bible shows how response is a part of the working of God. The separate acts of the creator each receive recognition: "And God saw that it was good." In this case it is still God himself who as creator voices this recognition. The goal of his creative acts, however, is that this recognition should come from the creatures themselves, and Psalm 148 expresses just this; in it, all creation in heaven and on earth is summoned to praise, "Praise the

Lord from the heavens—praise the Lord from the earth."[2] (author's translation)

Humanity is also included in this universal praise of God. The narrative of the creation of man in Genesis 2—3 ends with the expulsion of the man and woman, who have sinned against God, from the garden and thereby from proximity to God. But the woman, when she bears a child, gives her child a name which contains praise of God. So the first human birth praises the creator.[3] This one fact, which can be verified many times over in the Old Testament—that the name of a child contains praise—already expresses clearly enough that for the people of the Old Testament praise of God is an essential part of life. Thus a serious mistake was made in wanting to limit and restrict praise of God to the cult, as though praise were something which occurs only within the confines of a specific sector of human life, namely institutionalized worship.[4] But the Old Testament itself rules this out in that praise appears not only in the Psalms but in all the books of the Old Testament. It belongs to the whole life of God's people, just as it belongs to the whole life of an individual. This finds convincing expression in the words of Job. When he hears that he has lost not only all his herds and his servants but even his children, he says: " 'the LORD gave, and the LORD has taken away; blessed be the name of the LORD.' " (Job 1:21) No matter what happens in human life, praise of God must not cease. It cannot be stated more clearly that praise belongs to the entirety of human life, from beginning to end. Praising God and being a living creature belong together for the Old Testament, just as the sick king Hezekiah said after his recovery: "The living, the living, he praises thee, as I do this day!" (Isa. 38:19, author's translation)

Praise of God permeated the whole life of the Israelites; it was the natural reaction to events in which they experienced the gracious guidance of God. Therefore there is a natural similarity between the exclamations of praise in the historical books of the Old Testament and the expression "Blessed be Yahweh" in the Psalms; for instance, between 1 Samuel 25:32, " 'Blessed be Yahweh, God of Israel, who sent you to me this day,' " and Psalm 66:20, "Blessed be Yahweh, who did not take his mercy from me." (author's translations) Here we have gained an important insight pertaining to the praise of God in the

Psalms. It is a reaction to experiences gained outside worship in the daily life of the individual and of the community.[5]

This insight makes clear the difference between two kinds of praise of God, and hence between two kinds of Psalms of praise. The one type is a direct reaction to a specific, unique experience which is narrated in the Psalm of praise and which is therefore referred to as "narrative praise" (usually called "Psalm of thanksgiving"). The other type is not a direct reaction to a specific experience, but rather praises God for all that he is and all that he does. This "descriptive praise," which encompasses the fullness of God's work and being (usually called a "hymn"), is the specific praise of the congregation in worship.[6]

The simplest form of praise to God which speaks of an act of God is that of the exclamations we encounter in the historical books. These consist of an exclamation of praise together with a verb-dominated sentence narrating God's deed. The Song of Moses (Exod. 15), a song of the people liberated from the deadly threat of the Egyptians, comes close to this simplest form. The same structure is somewhat extended in the Psalms of praise of the people (Pss. 124; 129). This form is richly developed and expanded in the many songs of thanksgiving or praise of the individual, where the narration of the liberation is expanded by a retrospective view of past distress. This is one of the most firmly established forms of speech in the Old Testament. The report of distress, I called—he heard—he rescued me, comes after the call to praise and follows the praise of those saved. This sequence of sentences reflects the manifold experience of people who encountered the saving act of God, and who spoke about it to others. It is the original form of evangelism in the Old Testament.

This type of praise of God is, of necessity, characterized by verbs. What is said here originally about God is not a statement about God, but rather the narration of an experience in which a person was saved by God. This is the reason why a theology of the Old Testament must be characterized by verbs. Moreover, the character of spontaneity is important for this kind of praise. Individuals have experienced something which deeply moved them and which awakened joy, and so they must speak of it: explaining what God has done for them is a natural expression. In such a case, the strongest impulse to speak about God does not stem from a process of thinking or knowing; it does not come from tradition or because of an order issued by society; it comes from the heart which has experienced God's action. This is the source of praise of God in the Old Testament.

Finally, its public character is essential to this kind of praise. We encounter again and again in these Psalms invitations such as, "Praise the Lord with me. . . ." Genuine, living joy requires to be shared with other people, and because praise of God is joy verbalized, others are asked to share in it. The "imperative call to praise," which is so richly developed only in the hymns of Israel, has its roots in the invitation of one who has had an experience with God.

The other type of the praise of God, the descriptive praise (or hymn), expands this report of the one-time act of God; it praises God for all that he is and does. In these Psalms, God is praised with regard to the fullness of his working and his being. This is, therefore, the praise specific to worship and in which the entire congregation participates; in it is combined the praise of the saving and blessing God, the praise of the holiness and majesty of God, of the creator and Lord of history. It is in this type of praise that noun-form proclamation about God also has its place.[7] Hence, within it, the hymnic praise encompassing the working and being of God has many features which we also find in the hymns of other religions. In other religions too a god is honored in his majesty and goodness as creator. A peculiarity, though, of the descriptive praise of Israel, in contrast to the divine hymns of Egypt and Babylon, lies in the fact that it does not line up a series of various predicates of God, one after the other. Rather, it concentrates on a basic declaration, which in many Psalms forms the center of the praise, especially in Psalm 113 (author's translation):

Who is like the Lord our God, in the heavens and upon the earth?
who is seated on high, who looks far down . . . ?

These are two polar statements, out of which arises a movement: God is seated on high in order to be able to gaze into the depths from where the suffering people look up pleadingly to him. He is able to see into the deep because he has enthroned himself in the heavens, above all earthly events, and is thus able to oversee all things, but also to avert all suffering. This basic polar statement unites the descriptive with the narrative praise. Even when the hymn uses nouns to speak of God, not only as regards his actions but also his being, this noun-form speech is, in its origin, recognizably derived from speech dominated by verbs. Therefore one can only speak of God's mercy because it is attested by the experience of living people.

Through the use of many subtypes of the hymn, this fundamental proclamation is varied, extended, and united with liturgical acts, but remains basically the same. A typical feature of Israel's Psalms of praise is the imperative call to praise, with which the majority of the Psalms begin and which sometimes characterizes the entire Psalm, as in Psalm 148. It is a cultic summons to praise, in many cases probably spoken or sung by a priest; but it is based on a summons to praise— such as "Praise Yahweh with me"—which had, as its impulse, an experience of God's help. However, in the hymn this summons tends to extend itself: the kings, the people, indeed, the entire creation is called to praise. Because God is so great and so marvelous, the call to praise must go out to everyone and everything. This universal call to praise in the worship of Israel is one of the most important passages in the Old Testament, in which it looks beyond the activity of God with his people to his working in the wider horizon of the world and of all humanity.[8]

In the Psalms all scenes of daily life are encountered: the house and the road, the field and the workshop, the sickbed and the bedroom; everyday occupations like eating and drinking, sleeping and getting up, working and resting; all ages of life from child to old man and the forms of community: man and woman, parents and children, brothers and friends.

The history of the people of God forms an important part of the Psalms, from its beginnings until the time of the Psalm in question. The tribes are spoken of, the kings, victory and defeat, captivity and liberation.

And finally, what the Psalms speak of embraces the whole of creation: heaven and earth, winds and clouds, trees and flowers, animals and stars.

Reference must be made here to the relationship of the praise of God in the Old Testament to faith in the New. In the New Testament, the answer of people to God's action in Christ is faith; in the Old

Testament, faith is only spoken of in a few special contexts, but praise is spoken of continuously. In many respects, it has the same function that faith has in the New Testament. Both are in agreement that a "Yes" to God is intended, and simultaneously they acknowledge that God is both the savior and the creator, who holds past, present, and future in his hands.

2. The Lament

In the Psalms, the praise of God has as its polar equivalent the lament.[9] The one cannot exist without the other. Psalms of praise and Psalms of lament carry more or less the same weight in the Psalter. Both together represent the call to God. Just as praise of God is the human reaction to God's saving, blessing, protection, forgiveness, so the lament is the response to God's judging and punishment and—more than that—to the turning away of God which people experience as pain and suffering. Just as praise is the language of joy, the lament is the language of suffering; and just as we can express by "joy and suffering" human life as a whole, so praise and lament in the Old Testament mean human life as a whole, turning to God.

The place of the lament in the theology of the Old Testament is in the context of the account of the deliverance which became the basis of Israel's relationship to God. Whenever we ask what exactly happened when Yahweh delivered Israel from Egypt, we have to speak of the cry of distress; it belongs to the "historic creed" (Deut. 26:7) as well as to the book of Exodus (Exod. 3:7–9).[10] If a theology of the Old Testament attributes fundamental significance to the deliverance from Egypt, the cry of distress must also have significance, because it belongs to the events of the deliverance, though this has not been widely seen in Old Testament theology.[11]

In the Old Testament the call of distress or the "cry out of the depths" or the lament is an inevitable part of what happens between God and man.[12] But in saying this we have to distinguish the lament of affliction from the lament for the dead. The lament for the dead looks backward, the lament of affliction looks forward. In the lament of affliction, the sufferers reach out for life; it is the only possibility left for them as long as they have breath. In Hebrew, as in all primitive languages, the lament of affliction and the lament for the dead are designated by different words. Only the lament of affliction is directed towards God; the lament for the dead is a secular form (2 Sam. 1).[13]

The book of Exodus opens with a cry of distress; the call to God out of deep distress accompanies Israel through every stage of its history, as in the repeated phrase in the introduction to the book of Judges: ". . . they were in sore straits. But when they cried to the Lord . . . ." And thus it appears again and again in times of distress, up to the great catastrophe of the exile, when the laments of the book of Lamentations and many others brought before God the suffering of the nation. But the distress and the suffering of the individual also is expressed in the personal laments that pervade the whole of the Old Testament and form a part of the Psalter. "Out of the depths I cry to thee, O LORD!" (Ps. 130) And the Psalms of praise are reminders that God heard the lament.

Man as spoken of in the Old Testament is confined within the limitations referred to in the story of his creation in Genesis 2—3, the limitation of transitoriness and failure. The peril created by these limitations should and can be expressed in the lament; it is part of human nature that people can pour out their hearts in lamentation. There is a striking similarity between the distressful cry of the oppressed in Egypt and the wailing of Hagar's child in the wilderness (Gen. 21:16–17): "And as she sat over against him, the child lifted up his voice and wept. And God heard the voice of the lad. . . ." This is the function of lament: to implore God to be compassionate to those who suffer. All the multifarious forms of human affliction, oppression, anxiety, pain, and peril are voiced in lament, and thus it becomes an appeal to the only one who can alter the sufferers' plight.

The structure of the lament in the Psalms of lamentation reveals a transition. There is not a single Psalm of lament that stops with lamentation. It proceeds from address (sometimes with introductory petition) and lament to confession of trust, petition, vow of praise. In this structure it is evident that lamentation functions as appeal. The transition is already evident in the fact that the lament flows into petition; it is often indicated by a "but" *(waw adversativum)*, which introduces a confession of trust or some similar statement. At the conclusion of the Psalm, the transition is shown by a vow of praise or another anticipation of the saving intervention of God. Understood in this way, the structure of the Psalm of lament is one of the most powerful witnesses of the experience of God's activity in the Old Testament.

A characteristic of the lament is that it usually has three dimensions. It is directed towards God (a complaint against God), towards other people (complaint against an enemy), and expresses the lamenting person's own feelings (I-lament or We-lament) in describing the suffering. In these three dimensions the whole of man's being comes to expression. The lamenter is himself threatened by the power of death; he is threatened in his standing in the community, but also in his relationship with God. The threefold character of the lamentation shows an understanding of man in which the existence of an individual, without participation in a community and without a relationship with God, is unthinkable. It presupposes an understanding of man in which theology, psychology, and sociology have not yet been separated from each other. This corresponds exactly to the account of the creation of man in Genesis 2, in which man is created as an individual for fellowship with others and in relationship with his creator. The same threefold character forms the structure of the drama of Job between God, his friends, and Job himself.[14]

If we look at the subject of lament, we have to distinguish first between the lament of the people and the individual lament. This distinction is important for theology. The relationship between an individual and God is not the same as the relationship between a people and God. The lament of the people contains an important motif: the reference to God's former acts of salvation, as in Psalm 80. The awareness of the contrast between God's former and his present activity signifies an awakening of historical consciousness which begins to see history in a broader context. This is clearly expressed in the parable of the vinedresser and his vineyard. This parable presents history as a totality.[15]

The theological significance of the personal lament lies in the fact that it gives voice to all human suffering; suffering is given dignity by being expressed in words. It is something worthy of being brought before God. Thus, lament becomes a movement towards God. Understood in this way, the history of the lament in the Old Testament reaches its climax in the book of Job. His lament is the utterance of one who clings to an incomprehensible God. He clings to God against God. And the book concludes with the fact that God has heard him.

But the people and the individual are not the only subjects of lamentation in the Old Testament. There is the lament of the mediator, a rare but important intermediate form. It is a personal lament, but one which deals with matters confronting the people. It first appears in the lament of Moses, recurs in the lament of Elijah, and reaches a high point in the laments of Jeremiah, which, in turn, point to the Songs of the Suffering Servant in Deutero-Isaiah. The cry of Jesus on the cross stands in continuity with this history of the lament of the mediator as it runs through the whole of the Old Testament.[16]

The laments of Jeremiah attest the history both of the Psalms of lament and of the prophets.[17] In his laments, Jeremiah is simply a man who suffers and who speaks the language of his suffering people. But he is also a prophet who had been thrust into suffering by his mission. The history of the lament and the history of the messengers of God meet in the laments of Jeremiah. Between the suffering in the laments of Jeremiah and the suffering and death of Jesus stand the Songs of the Suffering Servant in Deutero-Isaiah. Here we find for the first time vicarious suffering. The Suffering Servant carries on the work of the prophets, but this is now extended to all the nations (Isa. 49:6). Therefore, the accusation of enemies recedes into the background; even the transgressor is included in the supplication of the mediator (Isa. 53:12). The Gospel accounts of the suffering and death of Jesus follow the Servant Songs point by point.

Finally, in the Old Testament we also find the lament of God. The book of Isaiah begins with God's lament over the rebellion of his people: " 'Sons have I reared and brought up, but they have rebelled against me!' " (Isa. 1:2-3) The same lament recurs in the book of Jeremiah (Jer. 8:5-7). It stands side by side with Jeremiah's own laments in chapters 12; 15; and 18. God mourns over the destruction of his people (Hos. 6:4). The juxtaposition of God's wrath and God's grief in these texts is virtually incomprehensible. The lament of God is only one of those rare and extreme possibilities of speaking about God. It enables those who are afflicted to hold on to God as an incomprehensible God; one who judges and who also mourns. The

God who becomes a man has to be understood within the horizon of a history which ultimately reaches the point where God, as the God of judgment, suffers for his people.

B. The Response in Action

Just as God's word and deed are both relevant in every relationship of God to man, the human response is not only in words but in deeds also; in both cases the whole being of God and the whole being of man are included.

1. The Commandments and Laws

The commandments and laws belong together in the context of the word of God. Moreover, they are also a part of the human response, especially that of Israel, because in the context of them Israel is shown how she can answer God through her own action.

a. The Connection with the Sinai Theophany

The commandments together with the laws are associated with the Sinai experience.[18] They can only become an integral part of the Pentateuch, of the Torah, through this association with the theophany at Sinai. We know that the laws in Israel had a long history; we also know that the series of commandments arose gradually. The Decalogue of Exodus 20 and Deuteronomy 5 carries within itself the signs of its gradual origin. The same holds true for the history of the legal corpus.[19] Thus the association of the commandments and laws with the theophany at Sinai gives them a greater significance. Why did this happen? Israel's worship, and especially its worship at the transition to settled life, is based on this Sinai theophany. Significant for the worship of Israel after it is settled is the new divine relationship of Lord and servant, which is distinct from that of the period of wandering and which corresponds to that of the enthroned king and his attendant servants. As described by the Priestly writing with the concept of *kabod* (Exod. 24:15–18), the majesty of the lord belongs to the God revealed at Sinai.[20] While the guiding God is the God who directs the way, or who commands departure or indicates a direction, the lord enthroned in majesty becomes the God who reveals his will through the series of commandments, and then through the laws and the collections of laws.[21] The people declare themselves ready to serve this lord, as the representatives of the people attest at Shechem (Josh. 24).[22] The commandments and laws explain how the people of Israel can serve their God. And then, a great arch spans from the first commandment, which bases the exclusive acknowledgment of one Lord upon the liberation from Egypt, across and beyond the series of commandments (the two tablets) which is linked to this basic command, to the gradually growing corpus of law which determines the epochs of the history of the Israelites. It spans all the way to the Priestly law, in which the law became an extensive cultic law, corresponding to the way in which the worship of Israel was established by the theophany, as the Priestly law expressly states in Exodus 24ff.[23]

b. The Difference Between Law and Commandment

When we consider this large complex of commandments and laws, we are confronted with a difficult question for the theology of the Old Testament. Throughout the entire Jewish and Christian tradition, this large complex is understood, interpreted, and judged theologically by *one* concept, that of the Law. The question is, can we continue to maintain that in the Old Testament commandment and law have the same theological meaning and can thus be brought together under the concept of Law?[24]

The texts of the Old Testament reveal a completely clear and unequivocal distinction between commandments and laws. The commandment—or prohibition—is a single statement in which God speaks directly to people: "Thou shalt not. . . ." The law consists of two statements, an assumed situation and a determination of the consequences: whoever does this and that—such and such a thing will happen to that person. The commandment is a direct proceeding between God and people, and in this regard corresponds to a commandment to depart or a direction to follow, in the pre-settlement period. In contrast, the law is not a direct word of God; in every case it is tied to human institutions, since punishment requires some agency to execute the punishment. Laws about slavery presuppose a specific social order. This is also the reason why the laws within the legal corpus of the Old Testament are much more subject to change than the commandments. The laws for sacrifices, for example, were bound to become inoperative when the temple was destroyed; the laws about slavery, when slavery was done away with. The commandments of the Decalogue, however, are not subject to such changes; commands such as "thou shalt not steal," "thou shalt not commit adultery" still stand today. This is also the reason why the Ten Commandments could be taken over by the Christian church and have retained their significance far beyond it.[25]

However, all this simply corresponds to the situation in the Old Testament itself: only in the Sinai account of the Decalogue does the word of God issue directly from the mountain of God to Israel; and the Decalogue in Deuteronomy 5 is definitely placed before the laws which follow in chapters 12—26. It was only in the late postexilic period that a comprehensive concept of the Law arose which made the commandment subordinate to the law. One can only conclude from this fact that commandments and laws do not have the same theological significance in the Old Testament. Only the commandment is the direct and immediate word of God; it was only subsequently that the laws were explained as God's word. In the Old Testament as well as in the New, the *commandment,* as God's instruction for human behavior, is necessary and indispensable for the relationship of God to man. This does not apply to the *laws* in the Old Testament in the same way. They are only necessary where they develop God's commandments and apply them to the various sectors of settled life; in the process they can change, and can even become inoperative.

In view of this situation, what Paul says in his letters about the Law must be reconsidered. He uses Law in the tradition of the linguistic usage of the late postexilic period, as a general concept for commandments and laws. The negative judgment of Paul concerning the Law can no more apply to the commandments of God in the Old Testament than it does to the commands and instructions of Jesus in the New. Speaking and acting are both the response of the person who has heard God's word and experienced God's action. It is on the basis of the instructions and commandments of God that a person can act.

If the commandments which God gave to the people of Israel extend their validity and their significance into our present age, far beyond the Jewish people and the Christian church, then we may regard this as a sign of the power and quality of God's instructions which have survived the changes of history.

2. Worship

Further, serving God has in the Old Testament—as in many other religions—the specific sense of worshiping God. Individuals can serve God insofar as they acknowledge God as their Lord in daily life, and do God's will; they can also serve God by bringing him an offering in the act of worship, at the holy place, at the sacred time. The institution of worship, however, is not solely concerned with the fact that people serve God with their offerings; it is rather that in the worship the relationship to God as a whole finds an institutionalized expression. All important parts of Old Testament theology come together in worship, which, therefore, really ought to form a special part of it.

In the Old Testament, worship is a reciprocal event between God and people. In it God acts and speaks, and people also act and speak.[26] This reciprocal event between God and people takes place at a special place at a special time, at the sanctuary on festival days. Since it happens at a special time and place, it is sacred; that is, an event removed from everyday life. As such, it requires a mediator of the holy, the priest. The worship of Israel in this form was established through the theophany at Sinai. Here, the group liberated from Egypt, on its way through the wilderness, experienced for the first time the holy place, the sacred time, and the word of God addressed to them in the theophany. Moses became the mediator of the holy in this event. What was established at Sinai was the worship of the later, settled form of life, as the Priestly writing shows: the tabernacle which God commanded to be built in the revelation at Sinai is the model for the temple.

3. Viewpoints for Understanding Worship in the Old Testament

a. Two Types of Cult

Worship in the Old Testament has a history. The most important caesura is the transition to the settled life. Only with this transition does the *Grosskult* first arise, in which a large festive congregation comes together in the sanctuary, the "House of God," on festival days. This is preceded by the early cult which we know from the patriarchal accounts, in which the congregation consisted of only a small family group, into whose life the cult was still fully integrated. In this early cult the holy place was not yet made by hands; it was the mountain, the rock, the tree, the spring. There were no priests as yet; the father received God's word and dispensed the blessing.[27] The second caesura is the establishment of kingship, which acquires major significance for the worship of Israel. The king himself becomes the mediator of blessing (Ps. 72), he dispenses the blessing (1 Kings 8); the priests in Jerusalem become officers of the king. The third caesura is the exile, introduced by the destruction of the temple. The offering of sacrifices ceases; at first, worship consists of nothing more than gatherings for lamentation, then a new type of worship by word arises alongside the restoration of worship by offering. In it, many features of the early cult come to life again, and the family regains a significant role in worship.

b. Blessing and Saving in Worship

The action of God in worship is, first and foremost, a blessing rather than a saving action.[28] The liturgical blessing, dispensed by the priest, is an essential part of worship; the blessing flows out from the sanctuary across the land. The constant character of worship, with its regular annual cycle of returning festivals, corresponds to the blessing. The blessing is vitally important to the everyday life of the congregation gathered together in worship. The saving action of God cannot take place in worship itself. But it is present in the service, on the one hand in the announcement of saving in response to the laments of the people and of the individual (the so-called oracle of salvation); and on the other hand in the word, in the remembrance of the saving acts of God in various forms, and above all in the association of the annual festivals with the working of God in the history of Israel.[29]

In addition to this the word of God has a decisive significance for the worship of Israel in the proclamation of the commandments, and in the representation of history in various forms and words which introduce and accompany the liturgical actions, as e. g., the words spoken for the dispensing of the blessing. How far the exhortation, as encountered in Deuteronomy, had a liturgical function is not yet certain. God's word in worship ought to be distinguished from the word of God to people outside the service—from, for instance, a messenger of God. Its peculiar character stems from the fact that, at a holy place and at a sacred time, it occurs against the background of quietness which hints at the presence of God, as the theophany in Exodus 24:15–18 shows. The willingness of the congregation gathered in worship to hear God's word is associated with this quietness. The possibility of the transmission of God's word is based on this peculiar character.

The human action in worship is the offering. Rather than go into the whole history of sacrifice,[30] I should like to make only two remarks about it: Although sacrifices were originally offered by the head of the family, the priest gradually takes his place. Although originally the offering had many different functions, in the later period the sin offering takes precedence; hand-in-hand with this goes a quantitative increase in sacrifices. The prophetic criticism of sacrifices is to a large extent caused by this trend.[31] What the worshipers say in worship is, on the one hand, the words which accompany the actions, which, like the sacrificial saying at the presentation of the first fruits, can be expanded into a creed (Deut. 26). On the other hand, there is the singing of Psalms by the congregation and by the individual, the meaning of which has already been discussed.

c. Worship as the Focal Point in the Life of the People

The relevance of worship in Israel lies in its function as the focal point of the life of the people. What is decisive is not what happens in the isolated service, but rather what happens in worship for the whole people and the whole land. Therefore, the walk from the house to the service, and from the service back to the house, is an important factor of the service itself. What is brought into the service on these walks from the outside life, and also what is taken back into everyday life from the service, are necessarily a part of the act of worship as well. Only in this way can worship be the center of the entire life of the people. Only in this way is criticism of worship also possible, as in the prophetic criticism of a worship which has become false. The reciprocal event of worship from God to people and from people to God receives meaning solely from the fact that it becomes the center of events outside the service.

d. The Universal Aspect of Worship

The Psalms show that in them the collective life of the community, and of the individual outside the service, extends into the service itself. Moreover, they show that worship in Israel had a strongly universal character. The praise of God has a tendency to expand. Even the kings and the nations are called to praise, and moreover all creatures, as is particularly evident in Psalm 148. Since the God of Israel is also the creator of heaven and earth, worship must encompass the entire span of creation. Looking back on the response of man in words and in action, we can see now how this response encompasses all of human life in speaking and in acting. There is a center of all the thousands of words each person speaks during life. This center is one's speaking to God, voicing the suffering, voicing the joy of life.

There is a center of all human actions throughout life, year after year, day after day. This center is one's doing the will of God, the obedience which seeks God's will, and the knowledge that worship can be the quiet center of all human activity.

VI

The Old Testament
and
Jesus Christ

To start with, a remark concerning method: in explaining this relationship it can be presupposed that each statement in the Bible may only be understood within its context. Since we are concerned with the relationship of the entire Old Testament to Christ, we ought to start from the context of the Old Testament as a whole, i. e., the canon in its three parts. It can further be assumed that this context is a historical rather than a theoretical one; both the Old and the New Testaments stem from a history that actually occurred. It is then not possible to have a comprehensive concept of this relationship according to which the Old Testament deals with the Law, the New Testament with the gospel; or the Old Testament with the wrathful, the New Testament with the merciful God. Such a concept is necessary, but it remains subordinate to the historical context.[1]

A. The Historical Books and Christ

1. The Saving God and the History of the Saved People

The beginning of the Old Testament tells the story of a rescue in the book of Exodus.[2] The beginning of the New Testament tells the story of a rescue in the Gospels. The prime declaration about God in the Old Testament, that God is the savior of Israel, persists even in the case of his relationship to the individual, as the Psalms demonstrate. Throughout the New Testament Christ is proclaimed as the savior; "there is salvation in no one else" declares the sermon of the first apostles (Acts 4:12). It is the saving God who acted in sending Christ. This, then, is a fundamental proclamation about God common to both the Old and the New Testaments. This proclamation of God as savior remains the same even though salvation in the Old and New Testaments may mean something different. The message of Christ as savior rests upon what the Old Testament says about God as savior. What is said in the New Testament about salvation from sin and death through the work of Christ would be incomprehensible without the experience of physical rescue from the danger of death. There would be no confession of Christ as savior from sin and death if there were no thanksgiving on the part of the person saved from the danger of death. Hence, even in the New Testament God remains the savior from the physical threat of death, as the accounts of the Gospels show.

If, however, the history of the saved people, or the history which grew out of the salvation process, is compared with the New Testament, then a very great contrast appears. In the Old Testament God's saving act inaugurates the history of a nation which, from the possession of the land up to the collapse, is based on political-military power, as one nation among others. In the New Testament, God's act of salvation in Christ establishes a religious or cultic congregation without any political power, made up of followers from many peoples, and similar to other cult-congregations within the Roman Empire.

This constitutes a definite contrast between the Old Testament and the New Testament which must be recognized. But the historical books of the Old Testament do not limit the history of God's people to the period of their existence as a state. Rather, they describe a history in various stages. The state of Israel is preceded by several different stages; after the end of the state a remnant continues to exist which no longer possesses the form of a state.

2. The History of Humanity and of a Family

The history of God's people is rooted in the history of humanity and in the history of the world (Gen. 1—11), from creation to the end of the world. This statement is common to both the Old and the New Testaments.[3] What is said in the Old Testament about God does not come to an end with the close of the historical books; and what is said in the New Testament about God cannot begin with the birth of Jesus. The working of the creator remains the same in both the Old and the New Testaments; God is just as much the creator for Christ or for Paul as he is for David or Isaiah. What is said in Genesis 1—11 about the relationship of God to the world and to humanity remains valid even after Christ's coming. The history of God's people in both the Old and the New Testaments is related to the history of the world and of humanity. In the Old as well as in the New Covenant God works not only for his people but for the sake of *all* men.

In Genesis 12—50, the history of a family precedes the history of the people. All types of community which are important in the history of humanity are relevant to the path of Israel through history; just as the history introduced by Christ is relevant, in the course of time, to all of these types of community. The family is of prime importance in this. It is for this reason that the patriarchal history belongs to the Old Testament. In it the whole of existence is defined by the communal form of the family, a pre- and a-political form of existence. The form of communal existence among the disciples of Jesus and among the first congregations is closely allied to this, as is the celebration of the Last Supper, the only form of cult in the Gospels. In the whole of medieval tradition the church was viewed only in relation to the state, and this was one-sided. The relation of the church to the family is at least equally important. What it means to be a brother in the Gospels can only be explained by the patriarchal history, even to the extent that a brother is prepared to suffer in the place of his brothers, as the Joseph story shows.

3. The Wandering People of God

God's message of salvation at the beginning of the Old as well as of the New Covenant sets his people in motion as the "wandering people of God." They are called out of their settled life to a life following the Lord. The wandering group of followers, which experienced the salvation from Egypt and was led through the wilderness, corresponds to the wandering group which was called out by Jesus and which followed him.[4] Despite essential differences, in both cases the followers are dependent for their whole existence upon their leader. In both cases, the experience of miracles, of rescue, and of preservation is part of following the Lord. The only command is the direction of the way, and the only sin is diverging from that way (as in John 6 at the end). In the Old Testament, the transmission of the wilderness wandering tradition was intended to leave open the possibility of a new call out of the settled life. This possibility was realized at the time of the exile. In Christian tradition, the concept of following the Lord has become abstract, which has caused differences in the forms of social existence to be considered irrelevant. At the same time, the concept is individualized, so that following the Lord becomes related to the personal piety of an individual Christian. In the Old as well as in the New Testament, however, following the Lord is only presented in terms of a communal form of life. It should be asked whether in Christianity as well as in the Bible, the act of following the Lord ought to be spoken of only in a specific situation where leaving the security of a settled life is demanded. In the history of Christianity such times have been of special importance: when Christians lived a life of following the Lord, this included a change in one's way of life.

4. Blessing in the Old and New Testaments

The transition to secure or settled life in the Old Testament has as its consequence a change in the way God works; God's saving work is combined with the work of blessing.[5] In the New Testament, this change is only hinted at; but even there the peculiar character of each type can be discerned. This finds expression in the ministry of Jesus; he works not only within the circle of his disciples, but also among the people in the cities and villages through which he passes. Keep in mind that Jesus really called only a few into his following. The others, for whom he worked, whom he healed, and to whom he spoke, he sent back home to their former life. A considerable number of the words and deeds of Jesus in the Gospels belong to the context of his work of blessing: Jesus is the encourager of those he meets in their normal life while he walks among them as healer, protector of life, and spiritual guide. To this same context belongs an essential part of the parables, which speak of the coming of the kingdom in organic images of growth and maturity, of seed and harvest. A conscious association of the eventful with the constant is revealed in the message of Jesus. The kingdom of God comes not only in events such as saving or conversion, but also in a gradual process of quiet growth. Both are bound up with each other in the life of Jesus as well as in his work and speech.

5. The Spirit of God

At the time of the settlement, the so-called charismatic leaders, the Judges, are the mediators of God's intervention on behalf of his people. The concept of the "Spirit of Yahweh" is encountered for the first time in their work.[6] The saviors of Israel are affected by this Spirit and given power to carry out the deliverance from their enemies. In the language of Christianity "Spirit" or "Holy Spirit" has become a one-sidedly static concept. The question ought to be asked whether more attention should again be given to the other meaning encountered in the stories of the Judges, according to which the Spirit of God is the enabling power for specific tasks in specific situations. In the New Testament, *pneuma* is understood in precisely this way in a very important passage, namely the story of Pentecost in Acts 2.

6. Kingship

Jesus of Nazareth received the title of Messiah, the Christ.[7] This royal title ought first to be understood within the context of the expectation of the Messiah at the time of Jesus and in the preceding period; behind this messianic expectation, however, stands the history of kingship in Israel from its inception with the promise of Nathan in 2 Samuel 7 to the end of kingship as reflected in Psalm 89. Out of this grew the expectation of another kind of kingship, of a kingdom of peace, whose king is a mediator of blessing (Isa. 9:1–6; 11:1–9; 32:1–8 among others). He will become king, not through battle, but rather by his birth. The promise of Nathan points to a hidden meaning in the gift of kingship which could not be fully worked out in the short history of kingship in Israel and Judah; hence the expectation of another king. But the title Messiah could only characterize the new kingship by a marked change, i. e., as the kingship of peace.[8] But the Suffering Servant in Deutero-Isaiah is much closer to the figure of Christ than the expected king of peace. This fact lies at the heart of the conversation with Pilate, in which Jesus in his answer to Pilate sees both functions combined in a paradoxical fashion: " 'You say that I am a king. For this I was born, and for this I have come into the world, to bear witness to the truth.' " (John 18:37)[9]

B. The Prophetic Message and Christ

It was the traditional interpretation that the significance of prophecy for the coming of Christ consists in the fact that the prophets had announced it; and the fulfillment that the New Testament announces confirms the promise of Christ in the prophets.[10] But this explains the significance of prophecy only to a limited extent—in terms of what the New Testament says about Christ; and it has nothing to do with the central task of the prophets, namely, the announcement of judgment on Israel. If there is any relationship of prophecy to Christ, then it must be explained in the light of the central function of the prophets.

1. The Prophecy of Judgment and Christ

The prophets were mediators of the word; they were powerless in their ministry. No single prophet attempted to exercise power in either a direct or indirect sense. In their duty as messengers, they had to make accusations against their people, and on the basis of these accusations announce the coming of judgment upon those people. The fact that they encountered resistance in this is understandable.[11] None of the prophets met with complete and thoroughgoing success in his message. The word which they had to announce was rejected. This rejection caused the prophets of judgment to suffer—by persecution, but also by the awareness of their lack of success (Isa. 49:4). It is this connection between the prophets' message of judgment and their subsequent suffering that points toward Christ. The deadly threat in the period of the prophets of judgment was not that of political enemies, but rather of falling away from God. But if the prophets' message of judgment died away apparently without effect, the suffering of the messengers of judgment gained significance. In the line of prophets, the suffering of the last in line, Jeremiah, stands out prominently; so much so that his laments (in Jer. 11—20) become a main part of his message.[12]

These laments continue in the Songs of the Suffering Servant in Deutero-Isaiah.[13] They announce something which up till then was not present in the Old Testament: the possibility of a new existence through the atoning suffering of an individual (Isa. 53). Whether the event is in the past, present, or future remains undecided. The redemption of the sins of the people through God's Servant points to an event which cannot be fixed unequivocally in the Old Testament. When the title of the Servant of the Lord is applied to Christ in the New Testament, then this justifiably corresponds to our present-day scientific understanding of these texts in Deutero-Isaiah. The representation of Jesus in the New Testament has its closest contact with the Old in this correspondence: between, on the one hand, the working of God's Servant solely through the word, his suffering until death, his confirmation by God despite death or through and beyond death, and, on the other, the suffering, death, and resurrection of Jesus. In Isaiah 52, the chorus of those affected by the suffering and death of God's Servant confesses that they at first falsely interpreted this new act of God as God's punishment. This shows that even then this new act demanded a complete change in thinking.[14]

But the Songs of the Servant are not a random prophecy in the Old Testament pointing to Christ; they are rather the final stage of the history of pre-exilic prophecy, and are understandable only within this context. This context is expressly hinted at in one of the Servant Songs, Isaiah 49:1–6. In this Song, the Servant complains that he has striven in vain to bring Israel back to God. This complaint points back to the apparently fruitless work of the prophets of judgment before the exile. The Servant of the Lord sees himself in the line of the prophets, even if he himself has another task. Despite his complaint, however, his task is even further extended: " 'I will give you as a light to the nations.' " (Isa. 49:6) The task is no longer limited to Israel. This corresponds, on the one hand, to the largely unrecognized fact that (outside the Servant Songs) Deutero-Isaiah has already announced an extension of Israel's salvation to the other nations; it corresponds, on the other hand, to the fact that the work of Christ is valid for all of humanity.

2. The Prophecy of Salvation and Christ

In the prophecy of salvation, no such unequivocal relationship to the person and work of Christ can be recognized. The prophetic announcement of salvation heralds an event which stands in a recognizable relationship to the situation in which the announcement is made. For this reason, the Immanuel prophecy in Isaiah 7:14 cannot refer to the birth of Christ. What is announced here by Isaiah is protection from the approaching enemy. The birth of the child is a sign which is supposed to confirm the fulfillment of this announcement.

A distant hint of Christ can be found in those oracles of salvation which announce something new that extends beyond the history of the people of God in the Old Testament. Thus Isaiah announces in an oracle of judgment a different future action of God dealing with the "scoffers who rule this people in Jerusalem": " 'Behold, I lay for a foundation in Zion a stone, a precious cornerstone, . . . "he who believes shall not be defeated." ' " (Isa. 28:14–22, author's translation) Following the judgment, obedience to God will be grounded in faith, as in 1 Peter 2:4–6. In another way, Jeremiah 31:31–34 points beyond the history of the people of the Old Covenant: God proclaims that he will make a new covenant completely different from the one broken by Israel. Even though, with the coming of Christ, not everything was fulfilled which is described here as the new covenant, one can still say that this message about the new covenant points to Christ. Nevertheless, neither of these two passages acts as a direct announcement of the coming of Christ.

Among the descriptions of future salvation in the postexilic period, the messianic prophecies require special mention.[15] They gained a special importance in the New Testament and in the history of

Christianity. But what is said in these messianic prophecies has little connection with Christ; suffering has no significance for the king of the era of salvation, and there is no mention of salvation through forgiveness. Here the king is much more a dispenser of blessing than of salvation. The Songs of the Suffering Servant in Deutero-Isaiah point more directly to Jesus of Nazareth than do the messianic prophecies.

3. Christ and the History of the Promise in the Old Testament

The main center of gravity in the relation between prophecy of salvation and Jesus Christ lies in the history of the promise as a whole, not in individual sayings which may or may not point to Christ. The way of the promise through the Old Testament begins with the promises to the patriarchs[16] and continues with the oracles of salvation spoken by prophets, known and unknown through the time of the exile and later on (see chapter IV). Understood thus, the manifold promises with manifold content are signposts on the way pointing to a future expected from the mercy of God. The meeting point between the Old Testament's prophecy of promise and its prophecy of judgment is the prophecy of Deutero-Isaiah, who is a prophet of salvation himself, but can be understood only in the line of the prophecy of judgment preceding him.

There are then three stages in the history of God's saving acts: the rescue in the beginning, founded upon the mercy of God towards his suffering people; the rescue from Babylonian exile, based on forgiveness in light of the preceding history of apostasy; the rescue from sin and death in Christ, which introduces the history of the new people of God, and which took place for the benefit of all of humanity. With the liberation of Israel from exile God's rescue was already divorced from political power; Israel was saved, but did not regain statehood. With the coming of Christ this separation of God's saving act from political power was reinforced.

C. Christ and the Response of God's People

The history recounted in the Old Testament is a history of interaction between God and man; the response of those for whom God acts and to whom God speaks is an integral part of this history. For this reason the Psalms are an essential part of the Old Testament, and one should perhaps ask whether in them, too, any relation can be found to what the New Testament says about Christ.

1. Psalm 22 and the Psalms of Lamentation

The Gospels' presentation of the Passion of Jesus shows an especially marked correspondence to Psalm 22.[17] The frequency of quotations from this Psalm shows that the early Christian congregations had observed a striking similarity between the two. If this was regarded in the New Testament and in early Christianity in the sense of a prophecy, it must nevertheless be asked whether, regardless of this view, an agreement still exists when the Psalm is understood not as a prophecy but rather as was really intended, as a prayer. In any case, this original meaning of the Psalm is implied by Jesus' cry from the cross, which is definitely a call of prayer (Ps. 22:1 = Mark 15:34; Matt. 27:46). In the Psalms the lament of being forsaken by God is an expression of grievous, inescapable suffering; the accusation of God very frequently expresses in the Psalms of lamentation what we, in secular language, call despair, the experience of the abyss of meaninglessness.

When Jesus employs these words on the cross, he enters into the manifold experience of suffering among his people. Thus, he is no more than a sufferer among sufferers. Jesus takes up in his lament the same language of pain which was shaped by many individuals in his people over many generations. He not only died for sinners, he died for sufferers as well. His work, all the way to this abyss of meaninglessness, was done for the sake of human suffering. The work and suffering of Jesus are not only a part of the history of the mediator, as we have seen in the context of prophecy; they are a part, just as much, of the long line of anonymous human suffering.

In addition to this, a whole host of quotations from Psalm 22 is encountered in the Passion narrative. It is thus made clear that the entire Psalm is being referred to by these individual quotations. Among the many Psalms of lamentation, this one is distinctive in that, in its second part, it develops into a Psalm of praise; the turning point in the suffering of the lamenting person finds expression in a praise of God which looks back upon the rescue from impending death as though it had already occurred. If, however, the structure of Psalm 22 underlies the Passion narrative of Jesus, then the sequence of suffering, death, and resurrection is to be understood as one single context; from the very first, the resurrection of Jesus must have been a part of the Passion story, together with the suffering and death. Hence, there never was a tradition of the suffering and death of Jesus without any indication of this turning point. The fourth Servant Song has the same structure; here, too, God's Yes to the Servant, even beyond death, follows the report of his suffering and death.[18]

The adoption by Jesus of the lament of the suffering people also caused a transformation, however. Christ also died for his enemies and pleaded from the cross for forgiveness for them; because of this request concerning the enemies, the request for the destruction of the unrighteous, which was an integral part of the Psalms of lamentation, is done away with. For believers in Christ, prayer against anyone is no longer needed.[19]

2. The Psalms of Praise

In the Psalms of praise one can recognize a relationship in form and content to what the New Testament says about Christ. A more formal relationship can be found in the Psalms of thanksgiving or narrative Psalms of praise. The experience of rescue has the same sequence of events in both cases. This is manifest in the structure of the Psalms. After the announcement (I will praise you . . .) and an introductory summary, comes the retrospective view of distress, and the report of rescue in three steps: I called out—he heard—he saved me. The Psalms close with renewed vows of praise and/or praise of God (e. g., Pss. 18; 30; 40; 66:13–20).[20] The songs of praise in Luke 1:68–79 and 2:29–32, in which God is praised as the one who sent the savior of his people, are similar to this structure. The equivalent in the hymns of the church is even clearer, as in Luther's Reformation hymn: "Now Rejoice, All Ye Christian People" which corresponds point for point to the narrative Psalm of praise, or "Sing Praise to God Who Reigns Above" (Johann Jakob Schütz). This equivalence confirms that in the Old Testament as in the New, God's saving act receives the same response.

An equivalent to the structure of the narrative Psalm of praise can also be seen in the construction of the letter to the Romans, although it must naturally be taken into consideration that the letter to the Romans is characterized by theological reflection.[21] It deals with God's saving act in Christ. After the announcement in 1:14–15 comes the introductory summary 1:16–17, the retrospective view of distress 1:18—3:20, and the report of saving in 3:21—8:39. The three elements of this report, I called out—he heard—he saved, characterize the seventh chapter. The similarity to the Psalms of praise is also shown in the final call of praise to God in the eighth chapter. The beginning of the section of exhortation, chapters 12—15, echoes the renewed vow of praise.

A correspondence based more on content is presented by the descriptive Psalms of praise or hymns. In them what the Old Testament says about the mercy of God is summarized. It is not a timeless quality of God, but rather what a person experiences in relation to God. Amazed and moved, the congregation praises the God who turns in grace from his distant majesty towards them. "Who is like the Lord our God, in the heavens and upon the earth? who is seated on high, who looks far down . . . ?" (Ps. 113:5–6, author's translation) It is this amazing joy at God's bending down to the depths of human suffering and human sin which finds similar expression in the New Testament in reference to the coming of Christ: " 'Blessed be the Lord God of Israel, for he has visited and redeemed his people.' " (Luke 1:68) The Christ hymn, Philippians 2, may also be compared with this. Once again there are the hymns of the church in which this note is taken up, especially the songs of the incarnation, the Christmas hymns. Christianity sees in the incarnation the ultimate revelation of God, who came down from the majesty of his divine being into the depths of human suffering and sin.[22]

A totally different relation appears in the imperative call of praise which either introduces the Psalm of praise or permeates it. It has a tendency to expand. At first, only the worshiping congregation is called to praise; then, however, all kings of the earth, all nations and parts of the earth, and indeed all creatures are called. God's work is so marvelous and so powerful that it must resound to the limits of all creation. God's act in Christ is spoken of in the same way in the book of Acts, and the missionary impulse is the same: to spread God's mighty acts over the whole earth.

3. The Response in Action: The Law

This element of the Old Testament—the Law—has been seen as decisive for the relationship of the Old Testament to Christ, particularly by Paul and after him in Christian theology. Indeed, it functioned as a contrast. It was rooted in Jewish theology in the centuries before Christ, this theology being the "spiritual homeland" of Paul, although it was not actually present in the Old Testament itself. Paul's contrast between the two ways of salvation, through works of the Law and through the saving work of Christ, has no foundation in the Old Testament. In the Old Testament there is not a single context in which the Law is depicted as a means of salvation. Usually Deuteronomy is cited in this connection: the obedience of the people to the commandments, rules, and laws is made the condition of Israel's welfare in the promised land. But in Deuteronomy observance of the Law is not tied to salvation, but rather to the people's well-being, namely the blessing in the promised land. The commandments and laws belong in the Old Testament to another theological context, that is, one of reaction, of obedience. The fulfillment of the commandments and laws is not an action which will achieve rescue or salvation, it is much more the action of those who have experienced God's salvation, as the structure of the book of Exodus points out. And besides this, Paul includes both under the concept "Law": commandments and laws together. We have already seen that this is not the case in the Old Testament itself: it draws the distinction between both very clearly; they have a quite different theological significance.[23] The existence of God's people rests, in the Old Testament as well as in the New, on the saving act of God; and likewise, in both cases, obedience to the commandments of God and of Christ respectively is part of the reaction of those who have experienced salvation.[24]

Conclusion: The Question of a Biblical Theology[25]

What we have found in investigating the relationship of the Old Testament to Christ are not relations or contrasts of a conceptual type but rather correspondences or contrasts which relate to a sequence of events, a history of God and humanity. This history, with which both the Old and New Testaments deal, exists in two circles: the wider, which stretches from the creation to the end of the world; and the more limited one, which is the history of God with a specific section of humanity, the people of God. The Old and New Testaments deal with the history of the wider circle: they both speak about the God who created heaven and earth and who ultimately leads the world and humanity to a final goal. And both deal with the narrower circle which has two sections, the first treated in the Old Testament, the second treated in the New. Both sections begin with a saving act that establishes the history of the saved people: this is indicated by the expression "Old and New Covenant." The history of God's people in the Old Testament leads away from power and to salvation on the basis of forgiveness. Salvation in the New Testament, which is salvation from sin and death, constitutes a new people of God composed of believers from all nations. This no longer exists in opposition to others, but *for* the rest of humanity, as was already said about the Servant of the Lord in the Servant Songs. The same transformation occurs in the case of the saving of the individual through God. Because Christ died on the cross even for his enemies, the charge of the pious against their enemies is dismissed. The saving of the faithful no longer implies death for nonbelievers.

This transformation can best be seen in a sentence in the Psalms of praise: "The dead do not praise the LORD." (Ps. 115:17) Death was definitely the borderline for the relationship between God and man in the Old Testament. Through the death and resurrection of Christ this has been changed; death is no longer the absolute end for the believer, the work of God is no longer finished by death. Only this background can show what the death and resurrection of Christ really means for humanity.

The saving acts of God are accompanied by his blessing, which includes not only his people but *all* men. Throughout the history of Israel and of the Christian churches the creator remains creator of heaven and earth and of all humanity. He holds in his hands all living creatures, from beginning to end. There are many relations and interactions between God's saving deeds and his blessing; the blessing God is the saving God and *vice versa*. But there could be no history of God's salvation either in the Old Testament or in the New, unless it was within the wider horizon of the history of creation and blessing, the horizon which connects beginning and end. There would be no savior without the birth of a child; there would be no Christian congregation without the continuation of generations through the centuries.

In the history recounted by the Old Testament a direction towards a goal can be seen which points to what the New Testament says about Christ. In the light of Christ a Yes and Amen are spoken to the Old Testament as the way which leads to this goal. At the same time, with Christ a No is said to that which, through the work of Christ, is overcome and now ended. Then the history of the church or the history of the Christian churches becomes a section of the whole history of God with his people which must be seen in the light of the entire Bible. What the New Testament says about Christ has essentially the form of a report or story: first in the Gospels, which lead up to the death and resurrection of Christ, and then in the book of Acts, which starts from the death and resurrection of Christ and is directed towards Christ's return, with which Revelation also deals. Here, too, there is a correspondence to the Old Testament which should not be overlooked. While the Old Testament points from creation, beyond the history of God's people, to the "center of time," the New points from the center of time to the end of time. Thus, Old and New Testaments belong together so that, side by side, they can report the history of God with his people and can place this history within the wider horizon of the history of God with humanity and with the world.

A question should be directed here primarily to the New Testament theologian, as to whether it is possible to return from an intellectual and conceptual structure of New Testament theology to a verb-dominated or historical structure to present what happens in the New Testament between God and man. The first step toward this would be the recognition that what happened is more important than what was thought about it.

If this basic verb-dominated or historical structure of what the Old and New Testaments say about God were recognized in Old as well as in New Testament studies, we could return to a Biblical theology which included the Old as well as the New Testament, and which was based upon both. It is my belief that a Biblical theology is necessary for the incipient ecumenical era of the Christian churches.

Notes

I. What Does the Old Testament Say About God?

1. Many of the following notes are given only in order to enlarge positions taken in these short lectures.
2. See the review by Ernst Würthwein, "Zur Theologie des Alten Testaments," *Theologische Rundschau,* N. F. 36 (1971):185–208.
3. Gerhard von Rad, *Old Testament Theology,* 2 vols. (New York: Harper & Brothers, 1962), 1:115. See also Rudolf Smend, *Die Mitte des Alten Testaments* (Zurich: EVZ Verlag, 1970); Gerhard F. Hasel, "The Problem of the Center in the OT Theology Debate," *Zeitschrift für die alttestamentliche Wissenschaft* 86 (1974):65–82; and Walther Zimmerli, "Zum Problem der 'Mitte des Alten Testaments,'" *Evangelische Theologie* 35 (1975):97–118.
4. In German: Wenn das Alte Testament das, was es von Gott sagt, in einer Geschichte erzählt, kann eine Theologie des Alten Testaments nicht eine gedankliche, sie muss eine Geschehensstruktur haben.
5. Gerhard von Rad, *Theologie des Alten Testaments,* 2 vols. (Munich: Chr. Kaiser, 1958), 1:126.
6. Retelling the Psalms would be impossible.
7. Brevard S. Childs, *Biblical Theology in Crisis* (Philadelphia: The Westminster Press, 1970), points to the relevance of the canon for a Biblical theology.
8. The previous history of Old Testament theology shows how difficult it is to write a really comprehensive Old Testament theology.
9. Gerhard von Rad, *The Problem of the Hexateuch and Other Essays* (Edinburgh and London: Oliver & Boyd, 1966), pp. 1–78.
10. Hans Walter Wolff, "Das Kerygma des deuteronomistischen Geschichtswerkes," *Zeitschrift für die alttestamentliche Wissenschaft* 73 (1961): 171–186. English translation: "The Kerygma of the Deuteronomic Historical Work" in *The Vitality of Old Testament Traditions,* ed. Walter Brueggemann (Atlanta: John Knox Press, 1975), pp. 83–100.
11. Gerhard von Rad, "Die Theologie der Priesterschrift" in his *Gesammelte Studien zum Alten Testament* II (Munich: Chr. Kaiser, 1973), pp. 165–188, esp. p. 187.
12. Claus Westermann, *Grundformen prophetischer Rede* (Munich: Chr. Kaiser, 1960, 1964). English translation: *Basic Forms of Prophetic Speech* (Philadelphia: The Westminster Press, 1967).
13. Claus Westermann, *The Praise of God in the Psalms,* trans. Keith R. Crim (Richmond: John Knox Press, 1965); idem, "Struktur und Geschichte der

Klage im Alten Testament," *Forschung am Alten Testament, Gesammelte Studien* I (Munich: Chr. Kaiser, 1964), pp. 266–305.

14. I understand the word "theology" in the simple sense of speaking of God.
15. Martin Buber, *Ich und Du* (1923) in his *Werke,* 3 vols. (Munich: Kösel-Verlag, 1962), 1:77–170; idem, *Schriften über das dialogische Prinzip* (Heidelberg: Lambert Schneider, 1954), reprinted in *Werke,* 1:291–305. On this see also Heinz-Horst Schrey, *Dialogisches Denken,* Erträge der Forschung I (Darmstadt: Wissenschaftliche Buchgesellschaft, 1970).
16. Claus Westermann, *Genesis 1—11* (Darmstadt: Wissenschaftliche Buchgesellschaft, 1972); idem, *Genesis,* Biblischer Kommentar I (Neukirchen-Vluyn: Neukirchener Verlag des Erziehungsvereins, 1966), 1:203–218 (hereafter referred to as *Genesis*).
17. Franz Hesse, "Kerygma oder geschichtliche Wirklichkeit?" in *Zeitschrift für Theologie und Kirche* 57 (1960):17–26; Gerhard von Rad, *Theologie des Alten Testaments* (1960), 2:7ff.
18. The classic representation is by Johann C. K. von Hofmann, *Weissagung und Erfüllung* (1841, 1844). What is meant by "Heilsgeschichte" is given in an abbreviated form by Franz Delitzsch in his commentary on Genesis (4th ed., 1872), pp. 277–284.
19. Karl Barth, "The Doctrine of the Word of God," vol. I of *Church Dogmatics* (Edinburgh: T. & T. Clark, pt. 1, 1936; pt. 2, 1956).
20. Claus Westermann, "The Way of the Promise Through the Old Testament," *The Old Testament and Christian Faith,* ed. Bernhard W. Anderson (New York: Harper & Row, 1963, 1969), pp. 200–224.
21. "Tradition" in the Old Testament has to be understood primarily as the process of transmission, secondarily as that which has been transmitted.
22. Such a general concept of revelation is presupposed, for example, in Ludwig Köhler, *Theologie des Alten Testaments* (Tübingen: J. C. B. Mohr, 1947), pp. 82–112.
23. Claus Westermann, *The Praise of God in the Psalms,* pp. 69–72. In contrast, Jörg Jeremias, *Theophanie* (Neukirchen-Vluyn: Neukirchener Verlag des Erziehungsvereins, 1965), does presuppose a general concept of theophany.
24. Because in the Old Testament the saving God and the judging God are always the coming God, this coming of God always has to do exclusively with saving and judging; never is the blessing God or the creator spoken of as coming.
25. Claus Westermann, "Die Herrlichkeit Gottes in der Priesterschrift," *Forschung am Alten Testament, Gesammelte Studien* II (Munich: Chr. Kaiser, 1974), pp. 115–137.
26. The distinction between *revelatio generalis* and *revelatio specialis* is not rooted in the Bible. See Claus Westermann, *Genesis,* 1:240–241.
27. Adolf Wendel, *Das freie Laiengebet im vorexilischen Israel* (Leipzig: Eduard Pfeiffer, 1931).

28. See the article "Gebet" in *Die Religion in Geschichte und Gegenwart*, 3d ed. (Tübingen: J. C. B. Mohr [Paul Siebeck], 1958), 2:1213–1217.

29. Claus Westermann, "Anthropologische und theologische Aspekte des Gebets in den Psalmen," *Liturgisches Jahrbuch* 23 (1973):83–96. Also in *Zur neueren Psalmenforschung*, ed. Peter H. A. Neumann (Darmstadt: Wissenschaftliche Buchgesellschaft, 1976), pp. 452–468.

To the answer in words one could add the answer in thinking. The verb *d b r* has the sense of speaking as well as of thinking. And in the Psalms speaking to God can change to speaking about God. Speaking about God is what we call theology (see note 14 above). And within the Psalms of praise as well as in the laments, one can observe speaking (and thinking) about God evolving from speaking to him (e. g., Pss. 30; 34; 39; 49; 90; 139). In the Old Testament, speaking to God precedes speaking about God. Understood in this way, theology and theological thinking in the Old Testament develops from speaking to God; it basically belongs to the human answer, to humanity's response.

In the Old Testament, thinking about God means, primarily, trying to understand what God does, what he has done. Trying to understand means interpretation. The Old Testament contains a wealth of theological thinking, beginning with short sentences of reflection in the Psalms mentioned above, and ending with such imposing theological works as that of the Yahwist, the writer of the Priestly Code, the Deuteronomist, the Chronicler, and many others. All these theological works reflect the story of God and man, of God and his people.

30. When in Joshua 24:19 Joshua says to the people, " 'You cannot serve the Lord . . . ,' " this is said from the viewpoint of the Deuteronomist referring to a specific situation; it ought not to be taken as a general statement.

31. Roland de Vaux, *Ancient Israel: Its Life and Institutions*, trans. John McHugh (New York: McGraw-Hill, 1961), pp. 415–423.

32. Claus Westermann, *Genesis*, 1:298–302.

33. Claus Westermann, "Creation and History in the Old Testament," *The Gospel and Human Destiny*, ed. Vilmos Vajta (Minneapolis, Minn.: Augsburg, 1971). The oneness of God is not a timeless doctrine in the Old Testament; the general concept of monotheism does not suffice to explain it. The fact that God is one is expressed in the Old Testament in different ways at different times. The most important stages are: (1) the first commandment, (2) the sh^ema' in Deuteronomy 6:4, (3) the message of Deutero-Isaiah. See Werner H. Schmidt, *Das erste Gebot* (Munich: Chr. Kaiser, 1970).

One may miss Wisdom in these outlines of an Old Testament theology. In my opinion, Wisdom does not belong directly to Old Testament theology, because Wisdom in itself is a profane genre, even if there are statements about God in the Proverbs. The connection between Wisdom and theology belongs to later stages within the Wisdom literature. The original place of Wisdom in what is said about God in the Old Testament is to be seen in connection with the creation of humanity; humanity is given the ability to understand the world and to find its way in the world. See my *Genesis,* 1:436–467 (on Gen. 4:17–26). See also Walther Zimmerli, *Grundriss der alttestamentlichen Theologie* (Stuttgart: Kohlhammer, 1972), pp. 136–146; English translation: *Old Testament Theology in Outline* (Atlanta: John Knox Press, 1978), pp. 155–166. Cf. my article, "Weisheit im Sprichwort," *Forschung am Alten Testament, Gesammelte Studien* II:149–161.

II. The Saving God and History

1. For the Old Testament theologies of Gerhard von Rad and Walther Zimmerli, the exodus event is always the starting point.
2. Gerhard von Rad, *The Problem of the Hexateuch and Other Essays,* pp. 1–78.
3. Cf. the examples given by Martin Noth, *A History of Pentateuchal Traditions,* trans. Bernhard W. Anderson (Englewood Cliffs, N. J.: Prentice-Hall, 1972), pp. 48–50.
4. Claus Westermann, "Vergegenwärtigung der Geschichte in den Psalmen," *Forschung am Alten Testament, Gesammelte Studien* I:306–335.
5. In reference to this and the following sentences, see the articles on the verbs *n ṣ l* and *j š ᶜ* in *Theologisches Handwörterbuch zum Alten Testament,* ed. Ernst Jenni and Claus Westermann (Zurich: Theologischer Verlag, 1971).
6. Claus Westermann, *Genesis,* pt. 2, Einleitung: "Die Religion der Väter."
7. It is this fact that has been obscured by the noun-form expressions. If one uses the term "salvation" *(das Heil),* then the difference is evident: salvation in the New Testament differs from salvation in the Old. But if one talks about God's *saving,* then what is common to both is evident: both the Old Testament and the New are talking about the saving God.
8. George Ernest Wright, *God Who Acts* (London: SCM Press, 1952). When, however, the Old Testament tells of blessing, then the emphasis is on the *state* caused by blessing.
9. In almost every newspaper, being saved is spoken of in this way. See also Thornton Wilder's *The Skin of Our Teeth.*
10. Leonhard Rost, *Das kleine Credo und andere Studien zum Alten Testament* (Heidelberg: Quelle & Meyer, 1965).
11. I also cannot agree with Martin Noth's opinion that the large themes of the Pentateuchal tradition have been summarized here (see note 3 above). The text of Deuteronomy 26:5–11 does not consist of a summary of themes, but rather describes a process in its individual stages.
12. The Sinai pericope (Exod. 19—24) cannot be fitted into this structure of events, as outlined so far; this has been shown by Gerhard von Rad and

others (see von Rad, *The Problem of the Hexateuch and Other Essays,* pp. 1–78). This pericope is based on the theophany, in which Israel receives the basic elements of worship as the sacred act; the laws and commandments are also attributed to this theophany. The covenant *(berit)* also belongs to this context, especially in Exodus 19:3–8 and 24:3–8. What has happened at Sinai between God and his people is stated in chapter 19 (without the later addition of verses 3–8) and 24:15–18 (P) without using the word *berit.* This word *berit* (covenant) is a later explanation of what had happened at Sinai. The word *berit* does not belong to the act of founding Israel as a people; it rather explains the state evolving out of this act. Its purpose is that of interpretation, but it does not originally describe the event of Sinai.

This is corroborated by the history of the word *berit.* Its original meaning is: a binding or solemn assertion (or obligation), so that, for example, a promise can be designated as a *berit* (Ernst Kutsch, article *"berit"* in *Theologisches Handwörterbuch zum Alten Testament,* 1:339–352). As such it can also designate a mutual obligation, as in Genesis 31:43–54. As a designation for the relationship between God and his people it is rather late, perhaps only beginning with Deuteronomy (according to Lothar Perlitt, *Bundestheologie im Alten Testament* [Neukirchen-Vluyn: Neukirchener Verlag, 1969]) and as an important theological concept within P, above all in Genesis 17 (Claus Westermann, "Genesis 17 und die Bedeutung von berit," *Theologische Literaturzeitung* 101 [1976]:161–170). For a review of the problem, see D. J. McCarthy, *Treaty and Covenant* (Rome: Pontifical Biblical Institute, 1963). For further literature, see Perlitt, *Bundestheologie.*

13. Ludwig Köhler, *Theologie des Alten Testaments,* pp. 54–58, has pointed this out.

14. Especially Gerhard von Rad and G. E. Wright (see his *God Who Acts*).

15. Bertil Albrektson, *History and the Gods* (Lund: Gleerup, 1967).

16. James Barr, *Old and New in Interpretation* (London: SCM Press, 1966).

17. Claus Westermann, *Genesis,* 1:606–614.

18. This corresponds to the relationship between the Deuteronomistic History Work and the Pentateuch.

19. See the article *"ruaḥ"* in *Theologisches Handwörterbuch zum Alten Testament,* 2:726–753.

20. As can be seen in the book of Lamentations.

21. Hans Walter Wolff, "Das Kerygma des deuteronomistischen Geschichtswerkes," *Zeitschrift für die alttestamentliche Wissenschaft* 73 (1961): 171–186. Also in *The Vitality of Old Testament Traditions,* ed. Brueggemann, pp. 83–100.

22. Cf. the introductions to the Old Testament, especially Otto Eissfeldt, *Einleitung in das Alte Testament* (Tübingen: J. C. B. Mohr, 3d ed. 1964).

III. The Blessing God and Creation

1. Claus Westermann, *Genesis,* 1:752–806; idem, "Die theologische Bedeutung der Urgeschichte," *Forschung am Alten Testament, Gesammelte Studien* II:96–114.
2. Genesis 1:26–27 gives the Biblical reason for human rights.
3. It is God as creator who gives meaning to life and death as the Bible understands these words; cf. the articles on *mut (sterben)* and *hajah (leben)* in *Theologisches Handwörterbuch zum Alten Testament.*
4. Claus Westermann, "Der Mensch im Urgeschehen," *Kerygma und Dogma* 13 (1967):231–246; idem, *Creation* (Philadelphia: Fortress Press, 1974). Originally, the question of creation and the creator was not an intellectual problem but an existential one: why is humanity so vulnerable in the world?
5. Claus Westermann, *Genesis,* 1:374–380.
6. The creation of man and the creation of the world originally were separate traditions.
7. Claus Westermann, *Beginning and End in the Bible* (Philadelphia: Fortress Press, 1972).
8. Gerhard Wehmeier, *Der Segen im Alten Testament* (Basel: Friedrich Reinhardt, 1970); Claus Westermann, *Der Segen in der Bibel und im Handeln der Kirche* (Munich: Chr. Kaiser, 1968); idem, "Blessing," *The Interpreter's Dictionary of the Bible* Supplement (Nashville: Abingdon, 1977); idem, "Der Frieden *(shalom)* im Alten Testament," *Forschung am Alten Testament, Gesammelte Studien* II:196–229.
9. Corresponding to the Hebrew *shalom* is the Latin *salus;* both are used for greeting.
10. Claus Westermann, *Genesis,* pt. 2, Einleitung: "Die Religion der Väter."
11. See chapter VI: "The Old Testament and Jesus Christ."
12. Ludwig Köhler, *Theologie des Alten Testaments,* pp. 54–58; and Johannes Pedersen, *Israel, Its Life and Culture* (first printed 1926; London: Oxford University Press reprint, 1953–54), I–II:182–212.
13. Gerhard von Rad, *Das Gottesvolk im Deuteronomium* (Stuttgart: Kohlhammer, 1929), reprinted in his *Gesammelte Studien zum Alten Testament* II:9–108.
14. For the religious festivals, cf. Hans-Joachim Kraus, *Worship in Israel* (Richmond: John Knox Press, 1966), pp. 45–124; and Robert Martin-Achard, *Essai biblique sur les fêtes d'Israel* (Geneva: Labor Fides, 1974).
15. It is therefore very strange that the relevance of blessing for the festivals, the processions, and the temple services is often totally ignored.
16. See chapter V: "The Response."
17. Claus Westermann, "Sacred Kingship," *Encyclopaedia Britannica,* 15th ed., Macropaedia vol. 16, pp. 118–122.
18. Claus Westermann, "Das Schöne im Alten Testament," *Beiträge zur alttestamentlichen Theologie: Festschrift für Walther Zimmerli zum 70. Geburtstag* (Göttingen: Vandenhoeck & Ruprecht, 1977), pp. 479–497.

19. On the following passages see Claus Westermann, "The Way of the Promise Through the Old Testament," *The Old Testament and Christian Faith,* ed. Bernhard W. Anderson, pp. 200–224.
20. Claus Westermann, *Isaiah 40—66, A Commentary,* The Old Testament Library (Philadelphia: The Westminster Press, 1966), pp. 269–299.
21. Claus Westermann, "Sinn und Grenze religionsgeschichtlicher Parallelen," *Theologische Literaturzeitung* 90 (1965):489–496; also in his *Forschung am Alten Testament, Gesammelte Studien* II:84–95.
22. Job for instance lives outside the land of Israel.

IV. God's Judgment and God's Mercy

1. Claus Westermann, *Genesis,* 1:374–380; idem, "Der Mensch im Urgeschehen," *Kerygma und Dogma* 13 (1967):231–246.
2. Very often the prophets point to this, above all in the contrast-motif; cf. my *Basic Forms of Prophetic Speech,* pp. 181–188.
3. *Basic Forms of Prophetic Speech,* pp. 169–175.
4. Hans Walter Wolff, "Das Kerygma des deuteronomistischen Geschichtswerkes," *Zeitschrift für die alttestamentliche Wissenschaft* 73 (1961): 171–186; also in *The Vitality of Old Testament Traditions,* ed. Brueggemann, pp. 83–100.
5. Cf. chapter II: "The Saving God and History."
6. See the article *"nabi"* in *Theologisches Handwörterbuch zum Alten Testament.*
7. Here the whole group of words pertaining to God's mercy or goodness has to be considered, e. g., *hesed,* in *Theologisches Handwörterbuch zum Alten Testament,* 1:600–621. The most important references are in the descriptive praise (hymns); cf. chapter V: "The Response." The praise of God's mercy, however, is a response to the merciful intervention of God.
8. Claus Westermann, *Die Verheissungen an die Väter* (Göttingen: Vandenhoeck & Ruprecht, 1976).
9. The mercy of God shown to an individual can be mercy on the sufferer (Ps. 113) or mercy on the sinner (Ps. 103), but the sinner is always a sufferer.
10. Rolf Knierim, *Die Hauptbegriffe für Sünde im Alten Testament* (Gütersloh: Gütersloher Verlagshaus G. Mohn, 1965).
11. Claus Westermann, *Genesis,* pt. 2, "Die Religion der Patriarchen."
12. Roland de Vaux, *Ancient Israel: Its Life and Institutions,* pp. 447–456.
13. Claus Westermann, *Isaiah 40—66, A Commentary,* pp. 130–133.

V. The Response

1. This may already be seen in the two meanings of the verb *bērēk.*
2. Claus Westermann, *The Praise of God in the Psalms;* and idem, *Genesis,* 1:238.

3. Martin Noth, *Die israelitischen Personennamen* (Stuttgart, 1928; reprinted Hildesheim: Olms, 1966), pp. 169–195.
4. See Sigmund Mowinckel, *The Psalms in Israel's Worship,* trans. D. R. Ap-Thomas (Oxford: Blackwell, 1962); and Erhard Gerstenberger, "Psalms," *Old Testament Form Criticism,* ed. John H. Hayes (San Antonio, Tex.: Trinity University Press, 1974), pp. 179–223.
5. Claus Westermann, "Anthropologische und theologische Aspekte des Gebets in den Psalmen," *Zur neueren Psalmenforschung,* ed. Peter H. A. Neumann (Darmstadt: Wissenschaftliche Buchgesellschaft, 1976), pp. 452–468. Also in *Liturgisches Jahrbuch* 23 (1973):83–96.
6. On the difference between praise and thanks, cf. my *The Praise of God in the Psalms.* For a different view, see Frank Crüsemann, *Studien zur Formgeschichte von Hymnus und Danklied* (Neukirchen-Vluyn: Neukirchener Verlag, 1969).
7. Here it can be shown that the verb form of talking about God is primary, the noun form secondary. In the descriptive praise of God's mercy, there is a gathering together of the experiences of those who, in the form of narrative praise, spoke of their experiences of God's mercy.
8. See chapter III: "The Blessing God and Creation."
9. Claus Westermann, "Struktur und Geschichte der Klage im Alten Testament," *Forschung am Alten Testament, Gesammelte Studien* I:266–305; idem, "The Role of the Lament in the Theology of the Old Testament," *Interpretation* 28 (1974):20–38.
10. See chapter II: "The Saving God and History."
11. Both praise and lament have a place in the Old Testament theology of Walther Zimmerli; but in that of Gerhard von Rad, there is room only for praise.
12. Cf. Claus Westermann, "The Role of the Lament in the Theology of the Old Testament," *Interpretation* 28 (1974):20–38.
13. On this difference, see *ibid.,* p. 22.
14. Claus Westermann, *Der Aufbau des Buches Hiob* (Tübingen: J. C. B. Mohr, 1956, 1977—gives recent literature).
15. Claus Westermann, "Vergegenwärtigung der Geschichte in den Psalmen," *Forschung am Alten Testament, Gesammelte Studien* I:306–335.
16. See chapter II: "The Saving God and History," and John H. Reumann, "Psalm 22 at the Cross," *Interpretation* 28 (1974):39–58.
17. F. Ahuis, "Der leidende Gerichtsprophet" (Diss., Heidelberg, 1971); John Bright, "A Prophet's Lament and Its Answer: Jeremiah 15:10–21," *Interpretation* 28 (1974):59–74.
18. W. Malcolm Clark, "Law," *Old Testament Form Criticism,* ed. John H. Hayes, pp. 99–139.
19. Martin Noth, *Die Gesetze im Pentateuch* (Halle [Saale]: Max Niemeyer Verlag, 1940), also in his *Gesammelte Studien zum Alten Testament* (Munich: Chr. Kaiser, 1957), pp. 9–141. English translation: *The Laws*

in the Pentateuch and Other Studies (Edinburgh and London: Oliver & Boyd, 1966), pp. 1–107.

20. Claus Westermann, "Die Herrlichkeit Gottes in der Priesterschrift," *Forschung am Alten Testament, Gesammelte Studien* II:115–137.

21. Walther Zimmerli, *Grundriss der alttestamentlichen Theologie,* pp. 39–48. English translation: *Old Testament Theology in Outline,* pp. 48–58.

22. See the articles on *'abad* and *šērēt* in *Theologisches Handwörterbuch zum Alten Testament.*

23. Claus Westermann, "Die Herrlichkeit Gottes in der Priesterschrift," *Forschung am Alten Testament, Gesammelte Studien* II:115–137.

24. This is the main problem with the fundamental work of Albrecht Alt, *Die Ursprünge des israelitischen Rechts* (Leipzig: Hirzel, 1934). English translation: "The Origins of Israelite Law," *Essays in Old Testament History and Religion* (Garden City, N. Y.: Doubleday, 1967), pp. 101–171. By using the same term, "Recht," for the two forms—apodictic and casuistic—he merely exchanges the governing concept of "Gesetz" for the governing concept of "Recht."

25. The specific meaning of the commandments finds a convincing representation in Gerhard von Rad's *Old Testament Theology,* 1:190–203.

26. In the well-known definition of Martin Luther, worship is represented as a reciprocal event between men and God. But this is limited to the spoken word.

27. Claus Westermann, *Genesis,* pt. 2, "Die Religion der Väter—der Gottesdienst"; Roland de Vaux, *Histoire ancienne d'Israel,* 2 vols. (Paris: Gabalda, 1971), 1:255–273; idem, *Ancient Israel: Its Life and Institutions,* pp. 289–294.

28. See Gerhard Wehmeier, *Der Segen im Alten Testament;* Claus Westermann, *Der Segen in der Bibel und im Handeln der Kirche.*

29. Robert Martin-Achard, *Essai biblique sur les fêtes d'Israel.*

30. Hans-Joachim Kraus, *Worship in Israel,* pp. 112–124; Roland de Vaux, *Ancient Israel: Its Life and Institutions,* pp. 415–456.

31. H. H. Rowley, *Worship in Ancient Israel* (Philadelphia: Fortress Press, 1967), chapter 5: "The Prophets and the Cult," pp. 144–175.

VI. The Old Testament and Jesus Christ

1. These questions about method are dealt with in Claus Westermann, ed., *Essays on Old Testament Hermeneutics* (Richmond: John Knox Press, 1963).

2. See chapter II: "The Saving God and History."

3. It should be recognized that the statements that God created heaven and earth and that he created human beings are more important than all interpretations of these statements.

4. Claus Westermann, *The Old Testament and Jesus Christ,* trans. Omar

Kaste (Minneapolis, Minn.: Augsburg, 1970), pp. 41–42.

5. See chapter III: "The Blessing God and Creation."

6. See the article on *ruaḥ* in *Theologisches Handwörterbuch zum Alten Testament;* and on *pneuma* in *Theologisches Wörterbuch zum Neuen Testament,* ed. Gerhard Kittel (Stuttgart: Kohlhammer, 1933).

7. Ferdinand Hahn, *The Titles of Jesus in Christology* (London: Lutterworth Press, 1969).

8. Sigmund Mowinckel, *He That Cometh,* trans. G. W. Anderson (Nashville: Abingdon, 1956).

9. See the commentary by Rudolf Bultmann on John 18:37.

10. Franz Delitzsch, *Messianische Weissagungen in geschichtlicher Folge* (1890, 1893).

11. F. Ahuis, "Der leidende Gerichtsprophet" (Diss., Heidelberg, 1971); John Bright, "A Prophet's Lament and Its Answer: Jeremiah 15:10–21," *Interpretation* 28 (1974):59–74.

12. Cf. chapter II, the section on the history of the mediator, pp. 35–36.

13. Sigmund Mowinckel, *He That Cometh,* pp. 187–257.

14. Claus Westermann, *Isaiah 40—66, A Commentary,* pp. 253–269.

15. Sigmund Mowinckel, *He That Cometh,* pp. 3–95; see chapter III, the section on kingship, pp. 48–49.

16. Walther Zimmerli, "Promise and Fulfillment," *Essays on Old Testament Hermeneutics,* ed. Westermann, pp. 89–122.

17. Claus Westermann, *Gewendete Klage, eine Auslegung des 22. Psalms* (Neukirchen: Neukirchener Verlag, 1955, 1957). See also John H. Reumann, "Psalm 22 at the Cross," *Interpretation* 28 (1974):39–58.

18. Whenever the accounts of the resurrection of Jesus have been isolated, the original connection between Passion, death, and resurrection has been ignored.

19. This is one of the most important changes in the relationship between God and man effected through the death and resurrection of Christ; its consequences have not yet been sufficiently thought about.

20. See chapter V: "The Response."

21. Claus Westermann, *The Praise of God in the Psalms;* idem, *Genesis,* 1:238.

22. The preceding passages may give a reason for the fact that the Psalms of the Old Testament could become a part of Christian worship; the New Testament does not include a book similar to the Psalms.

23. See chapter V: "The Response."

24. For the question of the theological significance of Law and commandments, it is again very important to know whether salvation is understood in a strict sense as a saving act of God or as a state of salvation *(das Heil).*

25. In the last few years a large number of articles have appeared on Biblical theology: Hans-Joachim Kraus, *Die biblische Theologie* (Neukirchen-Vluyn: Neukirchener Verlag des Erziehungsvereins, 1970); Hartmut Gese, "Erwägungen zur Einheit der biblischen Theologie," *Zeitschrift für*

Theologie und Kirche 67 (1970):417–436; Brevard S. Childs, *Biblical Theology in Crisis* (Philadelphia: The Westminster Press, 1970); James Barr, "Trends and Prospects in Biblical Theology," *Journal of Theological Studies* 25 (1974):265–282; and many others.